DINOSAURS
AN A-Z GUIDE

DINOSAURS
AN A-Z GUIDE

MICHAEL BENTON

Illustrated by

Jim Channell and Kevin Maddison

DERRYDALE BOOKS
New York

First published in 1988 by Kingfisher Books

Copyright © Grisewood & Dempsey Ltd 1988

This 1988 edition published by Derrydale Books, distributed by Crown Publishers, Inc., 225 Park Avenue South, New York, New York 10003.

Printed and bound in the United States of America

ISBN 0-517-66877-7
hgfedcba

Front cover: *Allosaurus*
Previous page: *Hypsilophodon*
This page: *Plateosaurus*

CONTENTS

INTRODUCTION   **6**

CLASSIFYING DINOSAURS   **8**
Orders, suborders, lizard- and bird-hips

THE HISTORY OF THE EARTH   **10**
How life evolved

DISCOVERING DINOSAURS   **12**
First finds and dinosaur sites

DINOSAUR COLLECTORS   **14**
A gallery of hunters

THE A-Z INTRODUCTION   **16**
How to use the guide

THE A-Z GUIDE TO DINOSAURS   **18**

DIRECTORY OF MUSEUMS   **166**
Where to see dinosaur displays

GLOSSARY   **169**

INDEX   **173**

INTRODUCTION

For over 160 million years the dinosaurs ruled the world. The last of these prehistoric reptiles died out 65 million years ago—many years before the first humans evolved about 5 million years ago. Dinosaurs were land-dwellers: some were so big that they would have stretched the length of ten parked cars, or been able to look over a three-story building. Others were no bigger than a turkey. In between were dinosaurs of all sorts and shapes, most of them completely different from anything we know today.

Dinosaurs were first collected early in the 19th century, and since then thousands of skeletons have been found. It is difficult to estimate how many species of dinosaur have been discovered. Early dinosaur collectors often named dinosaur species without checking if the skeleton really was different from all those that had previously been discovered. In some cases rival teams of bone hunters made up new names for everything they found. As a result of this confusion some species have two names—for example, the well-known dinosaur *Brontosaurus* should really be called *Apatosaurus* since this was the name given first.

Over the years, as many as 2,000 "species" of dinosaur have been named, but this number has been cut down to as few as 300 truly different species. Some of these are known only by a single tooth, or a small bone fragment, leaving about 200 well-known dinosaurs. Most of these are shown in this book.

Excavating the leg and shoulder bones of large sauropod dinosaurs at the Dinosaur National Monument, Utah.

How a fossil is formed

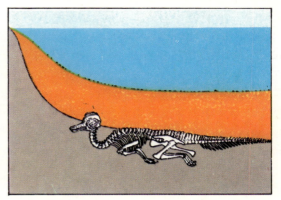

1. When a dinosaur died, its body might have lain where it would be eaten by smaller animals, leaving no flesh or bone. In other cases, the dead body might have been washed into a river or lake where it would sink to the bottom.

2. In a short time, the soft parts of the body—the skin and muscles—rot away, leaving the hard bones of the skeleton. If these were lying on the bottom of a lake, or in the bed of a river, they would gradually be buried by mud and sand.

3. In time the mud and sand turn into rock (called mudstone or sandstone). Chemicals in the rock pass into the dinosaur bones and fill up the tiny spaces inside, where they harden. This process makes a fossil bone heavier than a modern bone.

4. After millions of years the landscape changes, the river or lake bed rises, and the rock is worn away by rain and wind. The dinosaur is exposed on the surface and someone may find it. At first only a few fragments of bone may show, but dinosaur collectors are very skilled at working out what is beneath the surface, and how to dig it up.

CLASSIFYING DINOSAURS

When we classify dinosaurs, we try to decide how closely they are related to each other. The smallest unit of classification is the species, the largest unit used here is the order. In between there is a series of group names: suborder, infraorder, family, genus (plural: *genera*), and species.

As an example, how do we classify the big meat-eating dinosaur, *Tyrannosaurus rex (see diagram opposite)*? It is placed in the order Saurischia because it has a "lizard hip." It belongs to the suborder Theropoda, which includes all the meat-eating dinosaurs. Within this suborder, *Tyrannosaurus* belongs to the infraorder Carnosauria—the big meat-eaters—and is placed in the family Tyrannosauridae, with a few close relatives. Finally, the genus name is *Tyrannosaurus*, and the species name is *rex*.

Normally, when we talk about dinosaurs, we use only the genus name for simplicity, such as *Tyrannosaurus* or *Stegosaurus*. The species and genus names are written in italics, or underlined, to show that the scientific name is being used.

DINOSAUR HIPS
Dinosaurs are divided into two groups, or orders, the Saurischia (sawr-ISS-keea; lizard-hip) and the Ornithischia (orn-ith-ISS-keea; bird-hip). The Saurischia have the usual hip bone arrangement found in reptiles with each of the three bones pointing in a different direction. In the Ornithischia the forward pointing bone has swung around so that it points backward as well as forward.

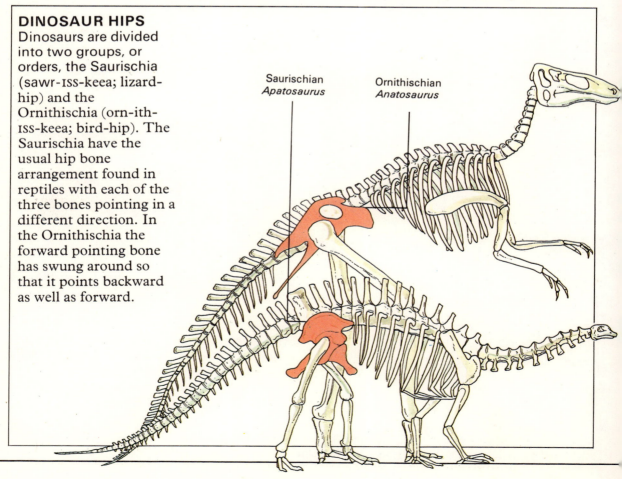

Saurischian
Apatosaurus

Ornithischian
Anatosaurus

Classifying *Tyrannosaurus rex*

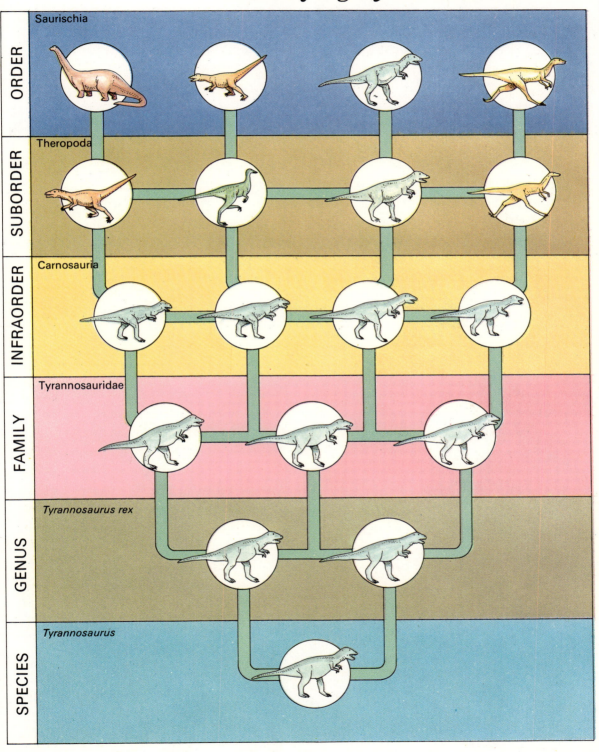

THE HISTORY OF THE EARTH

Dinosaurs are not the oldest known fossils—there had been a very long history of life before they evolved. As the chart on the opposite page shows, these early stages of evolution took longer than the whole period of evolution of more complex life that has followed since. This period of the first 4 billion years of Earth's history is called the Precambrian (pre-CAM-bree-an). The period of the evolution of more complex life after that—the last 600 million years—is called the Phanerozoic (fan-er-oh-zo-ic), which means "visible life."

In the Paleozoic (pal-ee-oh-zo-ic) "ancient life" various groups of animals and plants arose including corals, shellfish, insects, fish, amphibians, reptiles, tree-ferns, and conifers. Most of the important animals and plants in the Paleozoic belonged to groups that are now extinct. In the Mesozoic (mee-zo-zo-ic) "middle life" some groups typical of modern life arose, such as birds, mammals, and flowering plants. This was the age of the dinosaurs. In the Cenozoic (see-no-zo-ic) "modern life" mammals, birds, insects, and flowering plants were all widespread. Humans appeared only in the last few million years of the Cenozoic.

The Paleozoic, Mesozoic, and Cenozoic eras are divided up into periods, as shown opposite. The three periods of the Mesozoic, when dinosaurs ruled the Earth, are the Triassic (try-ASS-ic), Jurassic (joo-RASS-ic) and Cretaceous (cre-TAY-shus). At the beginning of the Triassic period, 245 million years ago, there were no dinosaurs. The Earth was ruled by several primitive groups of reptiles. These all died out about 20 million years later, and the dinosaurs rose to importance.

During the age of the dinosaurs, 200 million years ago, the continents were all joined together to form one land mass. The maps in the guide section *(see pages 18–165)* show the positions of the continents during the Triassic, Jurassic, and Cretaceous periods. The diagram here shows what happened as the Atlantic Ocean gradually opened up and the continents moved to their present positions.

1. Today
2. 100 million years ago
3. 200 million years ago

Time Chart

	Period	Description	Date (million years ago)
CENOZOIC 65–0	**Pleistocene**	The Great Ice Ages. First modern humans appear.	0 / 2
	Pliocene	*Australopithecus* appears. First cattle and sheep.	5
	Miocene	Many new mammals appeared. First mice, rats, and apes.	24
	Oligocene	First deer, monkeys, pigs, and rhinoceroses.	37
	Eocene	First dogs, cats, rabbits, elephants, and horses.	58
	Paleocene	Mammals spread rapidly. First owls, shrews, and hedgehogs.	65
MESOZOIC 245–65	**Cretaceous**	Dinosaurs died out. First snakes, modern mammals.	144
	Jurassic	Dinosaurs rule the land. First birds appear.	208
	Triassic	First dinosaurs, mammals, turtles, crocodiles, and frogs.	245
PALEOZOIC 570–245	**Permian**	First sail-back reptiles. Many sea and land animals die out.	286
	Carboniferous	First reptiles. Great coal swamp forests.	360
	Devonian	First amphibians, insects, and spiders.	408
	Silurian	Giant sea scorpions. First land plants.	438
	Ordovician	First nautiloids. Corals and trilobites common.	505
	Cambrian	First fishes, trilobites, corals, and shellfish.	570
PRECAMBRIAN 4600–570	**Precambrian**	• 700 first jellyfish and worms • 3500 Life begins in the sea.	4600

11

DISCOVERING DINOSAURS

Dinosaurs have been found in all continents except for Antarctica *(see map below)*. The position of these sites depends on the age and type of the rocks, and a lucky discovery by a fossil collector! New dinosaur sites are discovered every year, and there are clearly many more to be found.

The first dinosaurs were collected in the 19th century in England, often in old quarries, or at the foot of sea-cliffs. Dinosaur fossils were soon discovered in other parts of Europe and North America. During the 20th century large dinosaur collecting expeditions have gone to all corners of the world, and hundreds of tons of huge bones have come to light.

Between 1895 and 1905, the millionaire Andrew Carnegie spent 25 million dollars on large fossil collecting trips in the U.S. A complete skeleton of *Diplodocus* was found for him in 1899, and Carnegie had life-size casts made and sent to all the leading museums of the world.

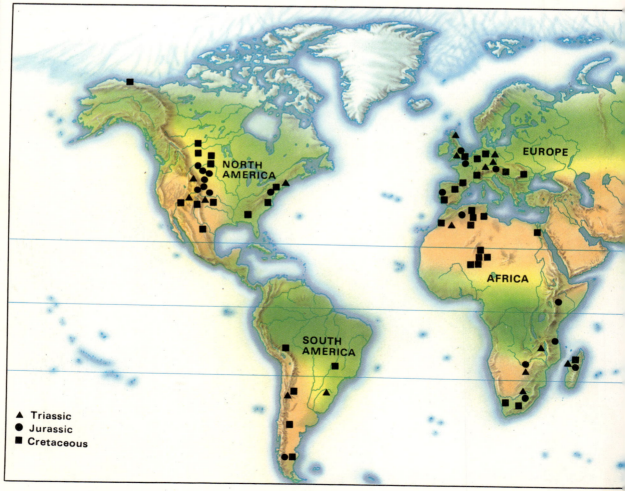

▲ Triassic
● Jurassic
■ Cretaceous

One of his collectors, Earl Douglass, found a remarkable deposit of dinosaur skeletons in Colorado, and in 1915 this was named the Dinosaur National Monument. The bone bed has been cleared, and visitors can now watch as the dinosaur bones are excavated.

Similar huge dinosaur deposits were discovered this century along the Red Deer River in Alberta, Canada. Barnum Brown and Charles Sternberg led two teams which collected hundreds of specimens between 1900 and 1920. A huge dinosaur collecting expedition began in 1907 in Tanzania (then German East Africa). The German geologist, Werner Janensch, worked there for four years, and sent 250 tons of bones back to Berlin, including those of the giant *Brachiosaurus*.

More recent finds have been made in Mongolia, China, Australia, and South America.

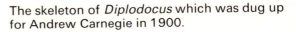

The skeleton of *Diplodocus* which was dug up for Andrew Carnegie in 1900.

13

DINOSAUR COLLECTORS

In 1677 Dr. Robert Plot gave the first description of a dinosaur. In his book, *The Natural History of Oxfordshire* he included a drawing of the end of a thigh bone of *Megalosaurus*: he said it was from a giant man.

Mrs. Mary Mantell found one of the first dinosaurs. She picked up a tooth of *Iguanodon* in southern England in 1822. Mrs. Mantell was an artist, and she drew pictures of rocks and fossils for her husband's books about geology.

Dr. Gideon Mantell wrote about some of the first known dinosaurs. He named the tooth found by his wife, and some other bones, *Iguanodon*. He collected bones and teeth in many parts of the south of England.

Sir Richard Owen invented the name "dinosaur" in 1841 for the six or seven species that had been named by that date. He helped to design some of the first life-size models of dinosaurs that were built in 1853.

Edward Cope was a brilliant paleontologist who named many of the new dinosaurs that were collected in the western U.S. At first friendly with Marsh, they soon became deadly rivals, and their dinosaur collectors often clashed.

Othniel C. Marsh was a professor at Yale College, Connecticut. Between them, Cope and Marsh named about 130 new species of dinosaurs from the western U.S. in the last 25 years of the 19th century.

This engraving, made in 1878, gives a rather simplified view of fossil hunting—dinosaur bones rarely spring from the ground with such ease.

Hundreds of different dinosaurs are now known, but this has not always been the case. Nearly all of the thousands of skeletons that fill our museums have been collected in the last 150 years. Before then, dinosaur bones were found but no one knew what they were, and scientists were very confused by them. They still thought that the Earth was only a few thousand years old, not thousands of millions *(see pages 10–11)*, and they did not yet know that animals could die out, or become extinct. The idea of a whole group of animals, such as the dinosaurs, that no longer existed anywhere on the Earth was quite out of the question!

Then two important discoveries were made in England. William Buckland, the Professor of Geology at Oxford University, received a small collection of bones from Stonesfield, a small quarrying village near Oxford. There was a jaw bone with long knife-like teeth, some limb bones, ribs and vertebrae. In 1824, Buckland published a description of these bones and named them *Megalosaurus* ("giant reptile").

The second dinosaur to be named came from Lewes in Sussex. It was discovered by Mary Ann Mantell. She was out walking when she spotted an enormous fossil tooth in a pile of rubble beside the road. She showed the tooth to her husband, Dr. Gideon Mantell, who was a keen amateur fossil collector. He found some more bones of the same animal nearby, and in 1825 named it *Iguanodon* ("iguana tooth"), thinking that it was a giant iguana lizard.

By 1841, another five or six species of dinosaur had been named, and Richard Owen realized that they were not simply giant lizards. He called them the Dinosauria ("terrible reptiles"). The study of dinosaurs had begun.

THE A-Z INTRODUCTION

The main part of this book is an alphabetical guide to all the important dinosaurs. Many of the names are made up of Latin or Greek words and are long and difficult, but they always tell you something about the animal—whether it was big or small, or whether it had big teeth or a long tail. Under the name of each dinosaur is a guide to how to say the names, and an explanation of the meaning.

Underneath this is the name of the person who gave the dinosaur its name, and the date that it was given. Then you will find some numbers, which, if you turn to pages 166–168 will tell you the names and addresses of some of the museums where a skeleton of this dinosaur can be seen on display.

The map shows the period— Triassic, Jurassic or Cretaceous— during which the dinosaur lived, and the approximate position of the continents during those periods (see page 12). The red dots show where remains of this dinosaur have been discovered.

The dinosaur silhouette shows its size relative to the dinosaur hunter— the length is shown in feet below. The color of the dinosaur tells you to which suborder it belonged (see color guide below).

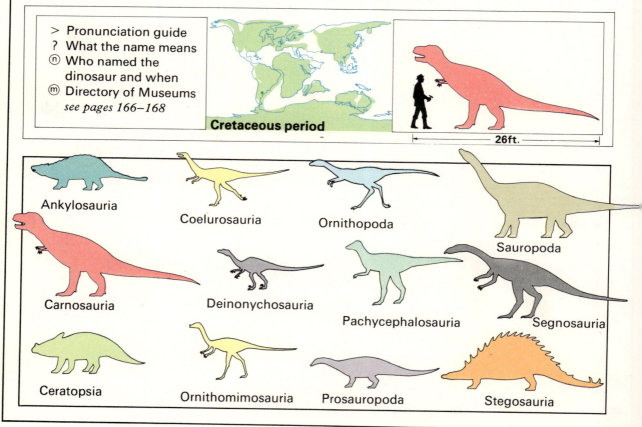

> Pronunciation guide
? What the name means
ⓝ Who named the dinosaur and when
ⓜ Directory of Museums
see pages 166–168

Cretaceous period

26ft.

Ankylosauria

Coelurosauria

Ornithopoda

Sauropoda

Carnosauria

Deinonychosauria

Pachycephalosauria

Segnosauria

Ceratopsia

Ornithomimosauria

Prosauropoda

Stegosauria

16

How the suborders are related

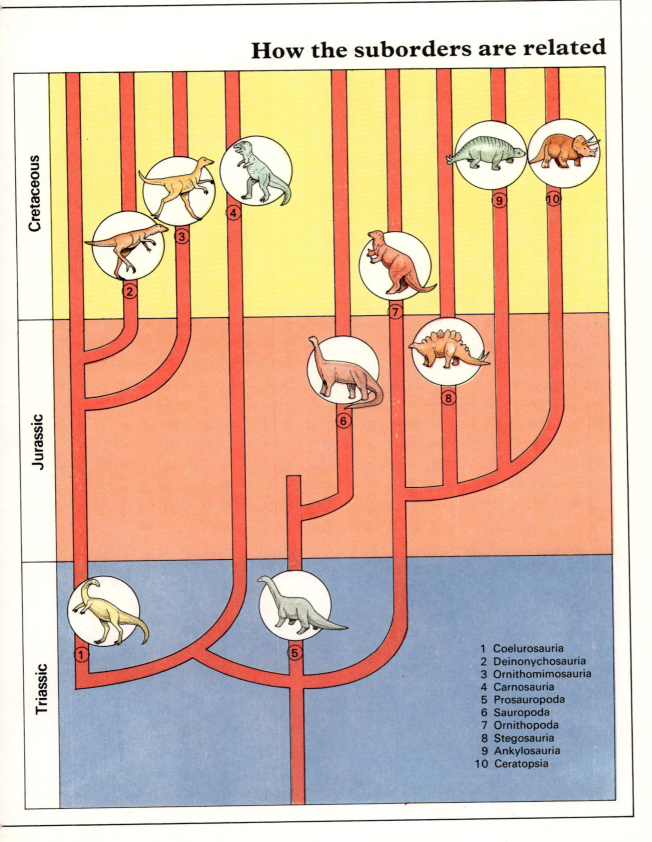

Cretaceous

Jurassic

Triassic

1 Coelurosauria
2 Deinonychosauria
3 Ornithomimosauria
4 Carnosauria
5 Prosauropoda
6 Sauropoda
7 Ornithopoda
8 Stegosauria
9 Ankylosauria
10 Ceratopsia

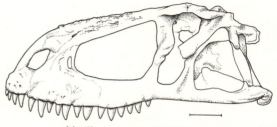

ABELISAURUS

> ah-BELL-i-SAW-rus
? Abel reptile
ⓝ Dr. J. F. Bonaparte &
   F. F. Novas (1985)
ⓜ

Cretaceous period

21 ft.

Abelisaurus was discovered only recently in Argentina. Its remains consist of an almost complete skull, but no bones from the skeleton have been found. The skull is very deep and has a huge opening in the side, just above the jaws. This opening is found in all dinosaur skulls, but it is rarely as large as in *Abelisaurus*. The eye socket is the tall, narrow opening behind this. The jaws appear to be very powerful, and the teeth would have been large and knife-like, as in *Tyrannosaurus*. The skull is nearly 3 feet long, which suggests that *Abelisaurus* had a long body.

Abelisaurus, although a meat-eater, is not obviously related to other meat-eating dinosaurs of the Late Cretaceous period, from North America or other parts of the world. For this reason it has been placed in a new group called the Abelisauridae. The only other known abelisaurid seems to be *Carnotosaurus*, which was also found recently in Argentina.

Abelisaurus skull (32 inches wide).

ACANTHOPHOLIS

> a-KAN-tho-FOLE-is
? Spine bearer
ⓝ Prof. T. H. Huxley
  (1865)
ⓜ

Cretaceous period

18ft.

Acanthopholis was a nodosaurid ankylosaur, a member of the group that includes *Hylaeosaurus*, *Nodosaurus* and *Polacanthus*. These all have quite narrow heads and a variety of bony plates and spines, and are more primitive than the ankylosaurid ankylosaurs of the Late Cretaceous.

Acanthopholis was an 18-foot long animal with an armor of rows of oval plates set in the skin, and sharp spikes along the middle of its back. The first specimens were collected in 1864 in an outcrop of chalk rock on a beach near Folkestone, in the south of England. These remains included three teeth, several fragments of backbone, part of the skull, some limb bones, and many small armor plates. Later finds in other parts of England added a little to these remains, but *Acanthopholis* is still only poorly known.

Acanthopholis

ACROCANTHOSAURUS

> AK-ro-KANTH-oh-SAW-rus
? Very spiny reptile
Ⓝ Drs. J. W. Stovall & W. Langston (1950)
Ⓜ 31

Cretaceous period

40ft.

Acrocanthosaurus was a large and terrifying meat eater about 40 feet long. Several skeletons of this animal were found around 1950. Some other skeletons from the same area of Oklahoma, were named *Saurophagus* ("reptile-eater"), but they may in fact be more specimens of *Acrocanthosaurus*.

The 12-inch spines on the backbone of this animal may suggest that it had a raised ridge or small sail along its back, similar to that of *Spinosaurus*. The sail may have been used to show to what species the animal belonged, or it might have been like the colorful feathers of many birds—a signal to tell rivals to keep away, or to attract mates. It might even have acted as a type of "solar panel," allowing the animal to control its own body temperature.

> AL-am-oh-SAW-rus
? Alamo reptile
Ⓝ Dr. C. W. Gilmore (1922)
Ⓜ

Cretaceous period

60ft.

Alamosaurus was a titanosaurid ("titanic reptile") sauropod, a group from the Late Cretaceous period which was found mainly in the southern parts of the world. Other titanosaurids include *Opisthocoeli-caudia* from Mongolia, *Saltasaurus* from South America, and *Titanosaurus* from South America and India. It is possible that some titanosaurids have been found in Europe, but *Alamosaurus* is probably the only find in this group in North America.

Alamosaurus was the last sauropod dinosaur, living right at the end of the age of dinosaurs. It was named after the Alamo, a fort in San Antonio, Texas near where it was discovered.

ALBERTOSAURUS

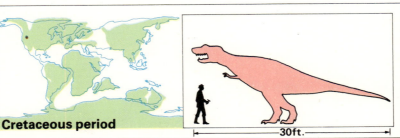

> al-BERT-oh-SAW-rus
? Alberta reptile
ⓝ Dr. H. F. Osborn (1905)
ⓜ 7, 13, 29, 30, 32

Cretaceous period

30ft.

Albertosaurus (sometimes called *Gorgosaurus*) also lived right at the end of the age of the dinosaurs. Dozens of bones and skeletons of *Albertosaurus* have been collected over the past 100 years, and these have often been given different names. One example of this is a small skeleton which was found in 1923. It was first called *Gorgosaurus* because it seemed very different from *Albertosaurus*. The body seemed slimmer, and the head was lighter. It has now been shown that this was a juvenile *Albertosaurus*, and that as the animal grew up it became heavier and stronger. This shows how careful paleontologists have to be when trying to name fossils!

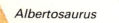
Albertosaurus

ALLOSAURUS

> AL-oh-SAW-rus
? Strange reptile
Ⓝ Dr. O. C. Marsh (1877)
Ⓜ 7, 8, 9, 11, 14, 16, 29, 30, 33, 35, 44

Jurassic period

40ft.

Allosaurus was the main meat-eating dinosaur of the Late Jurassic in North America. It may well have fed on such well-known dinosaurs as *Apatosaurus*, *Stegosaurus*, and *Dryosaurus*. *Allosaurus* probably found *Apatosaurus* too big to kill, but *Allosaurus* may have fed on its dead body because an *Apatosaurus* skeleton has been found with *Allosaurus* tooth marks on some tail bones.

The first specimen of *Allosaurus* to be found was a single broken tail bone discovered in Colorado in 1869. Of course, this was not enough to reconstruct the whole animal! Some more bits and pieces were found in 1877, and these were then named *Allosaurus*. A nearly complete skeleton, collected between 1883 and 1884, was called *Antrodemus* in 1920 but was later shown to be the same as *Allosaurus*.

Allosaurus

AMMOSAURUS

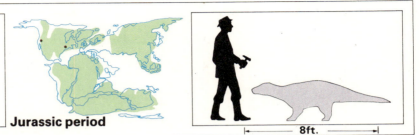

> AM-oh-SAW-rus
? Sand reptile
ⓝ Dr. O. C. Marsh (1890)
ⓜ

Jurassic period

8ft.

Ammosaurus was an 8-foot animal that could probably walk on all fours as well as on its hind legs. It is known from only a few partial skeletons which show that it was very like *Anchisaurus*. The first specimen was taken from a quarry in Connecticut 100 years ago while a bridge was being built. This bridge was recently knocked down, and more of the same skeleton was found in the rubble. *Ammosaurus* remains have recently been found in Arizona as well as Connecticut.

ANATOSAURUS

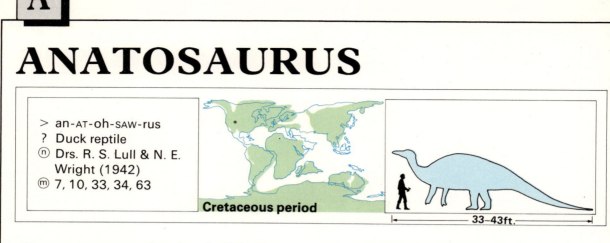

> an-AT-oh-SAW-rus
? Duck reptile
ⓝ Drs. R. S. Lull & N. E. Wright (1942)
ⓜ 7, 10, 33, 34, 63

Cretaceous period

33–43ft.

Anatosaurus was the classic "duck-billed" dinosaur. It had a low skull without a crest, and a broad snout just like a duck's beak. It was a large animal, up to 43 feet long. Many *Anatosaurus* skeletons have been discovered, some of which have been mummified, so that parts of the skin and even some internal organs have been preserved. From this paleontologists know, for example, that the bones of the hand were covered with a mitten-like layer of skin that joined the fingers together. This formed a webbed hand for swimming, just like the webbed foot of a duck. There were several species of *Anatosaurus* that lived through to the end of the Cretaceous period.

Anatosaurus

ANCHICERATOPS

> AN-ki-SER-a-tops
? Close-horned face
ⓝ Dr. B. Brown (1914)
ⓜ 24, 34

Cretaceous period

20ft.

Anchiceratops was 20 feet long with long horns above its eyes, but a short nose horn. It had a long neck frill with knobs and spines pointing backward, in the middle of which were two holes through the bone. These would have been covered by muscle and skin, and they may simply have been there in order to reduce weight. The pattern of the neck frill in *Anchiceratops* is different from all other ceratopsians, and may have helped the animals to recognize other members of their own species.

ANCHISAURUS

> AN-ki-SAW-rus
? Close reptile
ⓝ Dr. O. C. Marsh (1885)
ⓜ 5, 26

Triassic period

8ft.

Anchisaurus was a small, lightly-built animal, about 8 feet long. It had blunt, diamond-shaped teeth spaced out along its jaw, and could have eaten either plants or meat.

Anchisaurus had strong limbs and large claws on its thumbs which it could have used to pull leaves from trees, or to tear up flesh.

The first bones were collected in Connecticut in 1818, making *Anchisaurus* probably the first American dinosaur to be discovered. Some time later, similar dinosaurs were found in South America. At first these were called *Hortalotarsus*, but a recent study has shown that they belong to a species of *Anchisaurus*.

Anchisaurus

ANKYLOSAURIA

The suborder Ankylosauria is known only from a few rare fossils in Jurassic rocks. It was much more common in the Cretaceous, and especially later on, when many different kinds of Ankylosauria were widespread all over the northern half of the world. Ankylosaurs of the Cretaceous were most common in the Late Cretaceous of North America *(Ankylosaurus, Nodosaurus)* with rarer finds in the Early Cretaceous of Europe *(Hylaeosaurus)* and the Late Cretaceous of Europe *(Struthiosaurus)* and Asia *(Pinacosaurus)*. An important recent discovery has been the first ankylosaur from the southern part of the world, *Minmi*, from the Early Cretaceous of Australia.

The ankylosaurs were all plant-eaters, and they had an armor of spines, knobs, and spikes on their backs. This armor was made from pieces of bone that grew in the skin which formed a hard shell over the back and the neck, and would have protected the ankylosaur from the teeth of the meat eaters. Over the years, these simple bony plates became larger in some dinosaurs, and they grew out as great spines and knobs.

There were two groups of ankylosaurs, some with narrow heads and no tail clubs (the nodosaurids), and some with broad heads and heavy clubs at the ends of their tails (ankylosaurids). The tail club was an

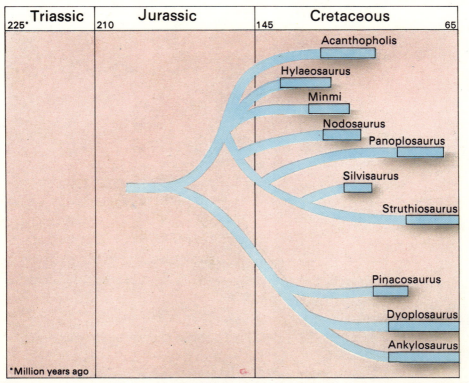

	Triassic		Jurassic		Cretaceous	
225*		210		145		65

Acantopholis
Hylaeosaurus
Minmi
Nodosaurus
Panoplosaurus
Silvisaurus
Struthiosaurus
Pinacosaurus
Dyoplosaurus
Ankylosaurus

*Million years ago

added protection against meat eaters for the advanced ankylosaurids: it could be swung from side to side with great force. Remember that the ankylosaurs were often very large: they may look like tortoises in illustrations, but they were often the size of a large car or a military tank.

Nodosaurus

Silvisaurus

Hylaeosaurus

Acanthopholis

Ankylosaurus

ANKYLOSAURUS

> an-KY-low-SAW-rus
? Stiff reptile
ⓝ Dr. B. Brown (1908)
ⓜ 57

Cretaceous period

35ft.

Ankylosaurus was the largest ankylosaur. It was over 33 feet long, and was the size and shape of a military tank. The body and limbs were powerful and protected by spines and bone plates. The tail was long and it carried a heavy mass of bone at the end. The tail club was formed from two expanded bones, one on each side of the tail bones.

This could be swung from side to side, giving powerful blows to any attacker. The muscles of the tail were well developed in order to use the heavy club most effectively. An armor of heavy bone plates and horns also covered the top of the skull.

The tail club of *Ankylosaurus* (club 16 inches wide).

Ankylosaurus

ANTARCTOSAURUS

> an-TARCT-oh-SAW-rus
? Southern reptile
ⓝ Prof. F. von Huene (1929)
ⓜ 17

Cretaceous period

60ft.

Antarctosaurus was probably one of the largest sauropods: its thigh bone alone was 7½ feet long, which is taller than the front door of your house. Its head was very small though—only 2 feet long. The skull was short, and low at the front, with eye sockets positioned at the back and nostrils on the top of the skull, between the eyes. There were only a few peg-like teeth at the front of the jaws. These probably acted like pincers which would pick up and snip off leaves. There were no teeth at all at the back of the jaws, indicating that the food was swallowed whole.

Antarctosaurus is known only from partial skeletons and single bones from many different countries in South America, and possibly also in Asia. It is probably closely related to *Diplodocus*.

APATOSAURUS

> a-PAT-oh-SAW-rus
? Headless reptile
Ⓝ Dr. O. C. Marsh (1877)
Ⓜ 7, 9, 11, 13, 25, 34

Jurassic period

70ft.

Apatosaurus is one of the best-known dinosaurs. It has been called *Brontosaurus* ("thunder reptile"), but the name *Apatosaurus* was given first. This was one of the giant dinosaurs collected in the "bone wars" in the American West at the end of the 19th century by Othniel C. Marsh *(see pages 14–15). Apatosaurus* had a heavy body and heavy legs, a long neck and tail. It was heavier than *Diplodocus* and not as tall as *Brachiosaurus,* two of the other well-known sauropods. Until recently, *Apatosaurus* was thought to be most like *Camarasaurus* because skeletons of *Apatosaurus* had been found without their heads, and had been reconstructed with a short skull. But in 1979 two dinosaur experts studied the field notebooks made by bone collectors a hundred years ago, and used these and other evidence to show that *Apatosaurus* had a long skull like *Diplodocus.*

Apatosaurus

AVACERATOPS

> AH-va-SER-a-tops
? Ava (discoverer's wife) horn face
ⓝ Dr. P. Dodson (1986)
ⓜ 6

Cretaceous period

8ft.

Avaceratops was named in 1986 for a partial skeleton of a small horned dinosaur that had been found in 1981 in Montana. The specimen includes most of the skull, most of the limb bones and a few bones from backbone and ribs. It seems to show similarities to *Brachyceratops* and *Monoclonius*. It had a short bony frill over the neck and a single short horn on the snout.

The small size of the skeleton (length estimated at 8 feet) is unusual. It has been suggested that this could be the skeleton of a young animal that was not fully grown, and that, even when it reached its adult size, it would have been smaller than its relatives. Recent collections at the *Avaceratops* site in Montana have produced 1500 bones of eight or more kinds of dinosaur, turtle, crocodile, mammal, and fish.

Avaceratops

AVIMIMUS

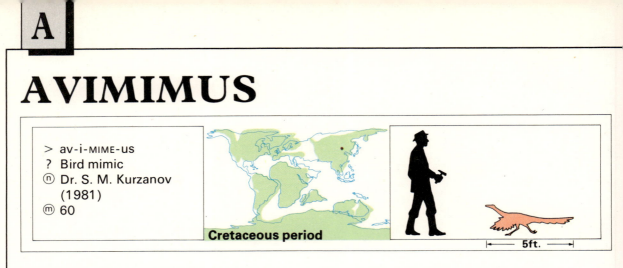

> av-i-MIME-us
? Bird mimic
ⓝ Dr. S. M. Kurzanov (1981)
ⓜ 60

Cretaceous period

5ft.

Avimimus was a small dinosaur, only 3 to 5 feet long, and very lightly built. Its legs are best known, and they have many bird-like features. In fact, the Russian scientist who described *Avimimus* in 1981 thought it was closely related to the birds.

BAGACERATOPS

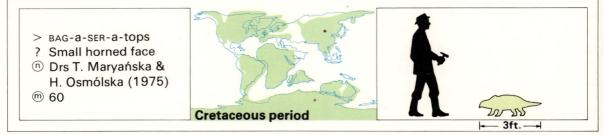

> BAG-a-SER-a-tops
? Small horned face
ⓝ Drs T. Maryańska & H. Osmólska (1975)
ⓜ 60

Cretaceous period

3ft.

Bagaceratops was a very small ceratopsian—only 3 feet long. It had a low neck frill, and a small horn on its snout. *Bagaceratops* had no teeth at the front of its mouth, but it had a tough beak with which it could have nipped off branches and leaves.

BARAPASAURUS

> ba-RA-pa-SAW-rus
? Big-leg reptile
ⓝ Dr. S. L. Jain (1975)
ⓜ 37

Jurassic period

60ft.

Barapasaurus is one of the oldest known sauropods. Its bones were found across an area of central India. When a huge bone was driven away, the driver called it a "big leg" in the local dialect—the origin of the name.

BAROSAURUS

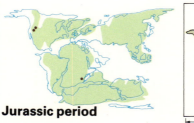

> BAR-O-SAW-rus
? Heavy reptile
(n) Dr. O. C. Marsh (1890)
(m) 35

Jurassic period

76ft.

Barosaurus is a very important dinosaur, because it has been found in the western United States and in Tanzania, east Africa, in rocks of the same age. This proves that this huge dinosaur could travel between the two areas and that they were joined together by land. It has been suggested that *Barosaurus*, and other large sauropods, used their long necks to feed high in the trees, just as giraffes do today. However, when *Barosaurus* lifted its neck the blood would have stopped flowing all the way up to its head, so it probably only lifted its head up for short times. The bones in its neck were about 3 feet long but were surprisingly lightweight. Each bone was hollow, and made from a narrow framework of bone struts. If the bones had been solid, the long neck would have been too heavy to lift.

Barosaurus

BARYONYX

> BAR-ee-ON-ix
? Heavy claw
ⓝ Drs. A. J. Charig & A. C. Milner (1986)
ⓜ 57

Cretaceous period

30ft.

One of the most remarkable recent dinosaur finds was a huge, curved claw, about 12 inches long, found in 1983 by an amateur fossil collector in a clay pit in southern England. The huge size of this fearsome claw showed that it must have come from a giant meat eater of some kind that had never been found anywhere in the world before. Further excavations at the site produced remains of the skull and skeleton, including half or more of the bones. These were enclosed in a very tough rock that has taken several years to remove. The claw of *Baryonyx* is remarkable enough—it was probably used like the slashing claw of *Deinonychus*—but it is still not certain whether *Baryonyx* had this claw on its hand or on its foot! The skull of *Baryonyx* is also unusual. It is long and flat like that of a crocodile. This, and the fact that fish scales were found in the stomach region, suggest that *Baryonyx* might have eaten fish.

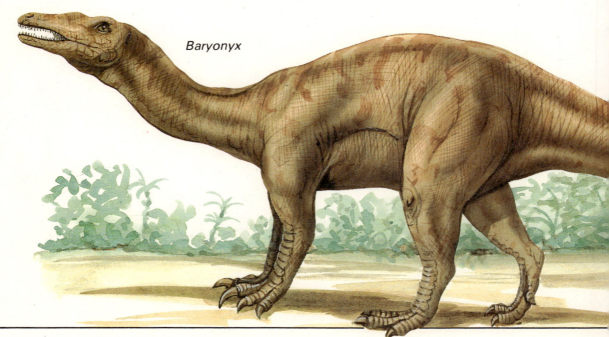

Baryonyx

BRACHIOSAURUS

> BRACK-ee-oh-SAW-rus
? Arm reptile
ⓝ Dr. E. S. Riggs (1903)
ⓜ 48

Jurassic period

74ft.

Brachiosaurus is the tallest dinosaur known from complete skeletons. It had very long front legs (hence its name, "arm reptile"), and if it stretched its neck upward it could have looked over the roof of a three-story building. The best skeletons were collected earlier in this century in Tanzania. Hundreds of local workmen dug the bones up by hand and carried them to a port to be shipped to Germany. Other specimens of *Brachiosaurus* have been found in the United States, but these are less complete. One huge skeleton of *Brachiosaurus* stands in the Humboldt Museum in East Berlin.

The long neck was made from 14 separate bones. Each of these had to be very strong in order to support the huge weight of the neck. There were hollow spaces in the sides of these bones which might have been filled with air spaces. Massive, rope-like muscles and tendons ran all the way down the neck and along the back. These were used to pull the neck up, rather like the steel cables on a mechanical crane. *Brachiosaurus* could probably have fed on leaves from tall trees, just like a giant giraffe! *Brachiosaurus* had its nostrils on top of its head, and it was once thought this was so that it could breathe under water. However, this is unlikely because the water pressure would have prevented it from breathing.

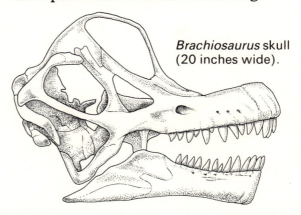

Brachiosaurus skull (20 inches wide).

BRACHYCERATOPS

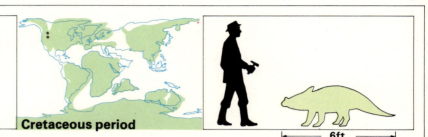

> BRACK-ee-SER-a-tops
? Short-horned face
ⓝ Dr. C. W. Gilmore (1914)
ⓜ 6, 30

Cretaceous period

6ft.

Brachyceratops was a very small ceratopsian, only 6 feet long. It had a well-developed, slightly curved horn on its snout and smaller ones above its eyes. The frill was short. *Brachyceratops* is known from five or six skeletons, all of which are young animals. It is likely that it was a young *Monoclonius*, but this is hard to prove.

The first specimens of *Brachyceratops* consisted of a fairly complete skull, and bones from other parts of the body, including the backbone, tail and hind limbs. The original skull was found shattered into many pieces within a small area of the rock. These had to be taken out separately, and then fitted together later in the laboratory.

BRACHYLOPHOSAURUS

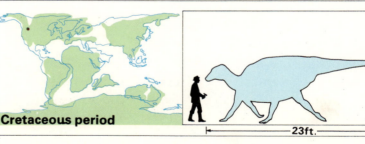

> BRACK-ee-LOAF-oh-SAW-rus
? Short-crested reptile
ⓝ Dr. C. M. Sternberg (1953)
ⓜ

Cretaceous period

23ft.

Brachylophosaurus was one of the most primitive duck-billed dinosaurs, or hadrosaurs. The first specimen, found in 1936 in the rich dinosaur beds of Alberta, Canada, was a skull and the front part of a skeleton (neck, shoulder region, and arms). The beautifully-preserved skull has a deep snout region with huge nostril openings on each side. Running back

from this is a simple crest made from the nasal bones, which extend between the eyes to form a broad plate. There is a little spike pointing backward. The crest was solid in *Brachylophosaurus*, and its exact purpose is hard to decide. It may have been a kind of identification signal to let other dinosaurs know what kind of dinosaur it was.

CAMARASAURUS

> kam-AR-a-SAW-rus
? Chambered reptile
ⓝ Dr. E. D. Cope (1877)
ⓜ 9, 11, 25, 30

Jurassic period

60ft.

Camarasaurus was a heavily-built sauropod with a shorter tail and neck than *Apatosaurus* or *Diplodocus*. Its head was short and it had a blunt snout. Its nostrils were on top of its head and this has led people to suggest that it could have lived in water. Its whole body and head could have been submerged with just the nostrils showing. The skull is relatively short and deep, and the eye sockets are large. The brain, however, was tiny, and filled only a very small space at the back of the skull.

Camarasaurus had long, blunt teeth which pointed forward. It probably used these to seize large mouthfuls of soft plants and leaves. The neck of *Camarasaurus* was shorter than in typical sauropods, such as *Apatosaurus* and *Diplodocus*, consisting of only 12 short neck bones. The feet were huge, in order to support the weight of the body, with claws on some of the toes.

Camarasaurus

CAMPTOSAURUS

> KAMP-toe-SAW-rus
? Flexible reptile
ⓝ Dr. O. C. Marsh
(1885)
ⓜ 7, 9, 11, 14, 16, 25, 29, 30, 35, 59

Jurassic period

21 ft.

Camptosaurus was heavily built and up to 21 feet long. It was similar in many respects to *Iguanodon*. *Camptosaurus* had long powerful hind legs and much shorter arms. However, it had small hooves on each finger of the hand, which shows that it walked on all fours at least some of the time. With its rows of hundreds of teeth, *Camptosaurus* could eat very tough plant foot. About ten species of *Camptosaurus* from different parts of Europe and North America have been described. These all differ in size and proportion, but show how widespread this one dinosaur was.

Camptosaurus

CARCHARODONTOSAURUS

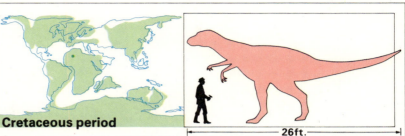

> kar-KAR-oh-DONT-oh-SAW-rus
? *Carcharodon* (a giant shark) reptile
ⓝ Dr. E. Stromer (1931)
ⓜ

Cretaceous period

26ft.

Carcharodontosaurus was a giant meat eater, 26 feet long. It may have fed on plant eaters that lived in the same area, such as *Ouranosaurus*. *Carcharodontosaurus* is known from a large number of specimens found in desert regions of north Africa, but none of the remains is very complete. There are parts of the skull, numerous teeth (some 5 to 6 inches in length), parts of the backbone, limb bones, and other fragments.

Carcharodontosaurus had short arms with powerful claws. At first it was thought to be a species of *Megalosaurus*, but it was later given a new name since the remains were rather different from that English dinosaur. Over the years, specimens of *Carcharodontosaurus* have been reported from many places in Morocco, Sahara, Niger, and Egypt.

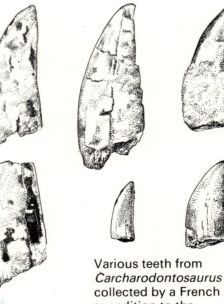

Various teeth from *Carcharodontosaurus* collected by a French expedition to the Sahara Desert in the 1950s (teeth range from 2½ to 4 inches long).

39

CARNOSAURIA

Tyrannosaurus

Megalosaurus

Allosaurus

Spinosaurus

Ceratosaurus

The infraorder Carnosauria includes all the giant meat-eating dinosaurs. The classification of this group is very difficult, but there seem to have been four main families. The biggest one was the Megalosauridae, which lived from Early Jurassic times right through into the Late Cretaceous. The megalosaurids are known almost entirely from Europe *(Megalosaurus)*, and North America *(Allosaurus, Dryptosaurus)* with rare specimens from Africa *(Carcharodontosaurus)* and recent important discoveries from South America *(Piatnitzkysaurus)* and China *(Xuanhanosaurus)*.

The three other carnosaur families are easier to define. The Spinosauridae had "sails" on their backs. This group includes *Acrocanthosaurus* from North America and *Spinosaurus* from Africa, both dating from the Early Cretaceous. The Tyrannosauridae were large meat-eaters from the Late Cretaceous of North America *(Albertosaurus, Daspletosaurus, Tyrannosaurus)*, Mongolia *(Tarbosaurus)*, and India *(Indosuchus)*. These all had powerful jaws lined with massive teeth and short arms. The fourth carnosaur family, discovered only recently, is the Abelisauridae from the Late Cretaceous of South America *(Abelisaurus, Carnotosaurus)*. Dinosaurs in this group were like the Tyrannosauridae in some respects.

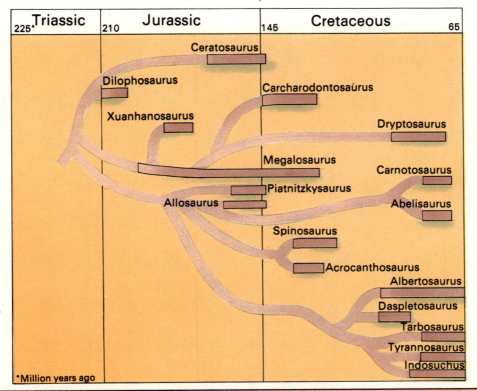

CERATOPSIA

The infraorder Ceratopsia includes all of the horned dinosaurs. This was a remarkably successful dinosaur group, although it was also one of the shortest-lived. Most of the ceratopsians lived during the Late Cretaceous period, the last part of the age of the dinosaurs; nevertheless they became very common and many dozens of species arose. Despite the many different kinds of ceratopsians, they have only been found in North America and Asia.

There were two primitive families (psittacosaurids and protoceratopsids) and a large advanced family (ceratopsids). The family Ceratopsidae is hard to divide up, but many paleontologists believe that

there were two groups in it: the "short-frilled" ceratopsids (*Avaceratops, Brachyceratops, Monoclonius, Pachyrhinosaurus, Styracosaurus,* and *Triceratops*), and the "long-frilled" ceratopsids (*Anchiceratops, Chasmosaurus, Pentaceratops,* and *Torosaurus*). The long-frilled forms seem to be more advanced in general than the short-frilled ones, and they occurred a little later in the Late Cretaceous, right before the end of the age of the dinosaurs.

The ceratopsians all had horns on their noses and above their eyes, and a bony frill running back from the head over the neck. The early forms, like *Psittacosaurus* and *Protoceratops* had

225·Triassic	210 Jurassic	145 Cretaceous 65
		Psittacosaurus
		Leptoceratops
		Bagaceratops
		Protoceratops
		Pachyrhinosaurus
		Brachyceratops
		Avaceratops
		Monoclonius
		Styracosaurus
		Triceratops
		Pentaceratops
		Anchiceratops
		Chasmosaurus
		Torosaurus
*Million years ago		

only thickened knobs of bone in place of the horns and very slight frills, and they represent an early evolutionary state. The other obvious feature of ceratopsians was the curved bony beak at the front of the upper jaw which allowed them to snip off bunches of tough leaves.

Pentaceratops

Styracosaurus

Triceratops

Psittacosaurus

Protoceratops

43

CERATOSAURUS

> SER-a-toe-SAW-rus
? Horned reptile
Ⓝ Dr. O. C. Marsh (1884)
Ⓜ 11

Jurassic period

20ft.

Ceratosaurus was one of the most unusual meat-eating dinosaurs. It was quite large, up to 20 feet long, and it had massive, sharp fangs. It also had a horn on its nose. This was probably not for self-protection, but it may have been used by males when fighting for a mate.

The first skeleton of *Ceratosaurus* was found in the same quarry as one of *Allosaurus*. *Ceratosaurus* was smaller than *Allosaurus*, but it had more massive jaws. Its hand had four fingers, while that of *Allosaurus* had only three.

Ceratosaurus

CETIOSAURUS

> SEET-ee-oh-SAW-rus
? Whale reptile
ⓝ Sir Richard Owen
  (1841)
ⓜ 3, 53, 59

Jurassic period

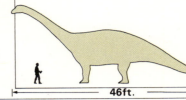

46ft.

Cetiosaurus was one of the earliest dinosaurs to be discovered: it was named in 1841 from odd teeth and bones. A partial skeleton was found in 1870 near Oxford, but a more complete skeleton was found more recently in Rutland, England, and can be seen in Leicester Museum. A thigh bone found in Morocco in 1979 was 6 feet long, the height of a tall man. *Cetiosaurus* was one of the earliest sauropods and it was primitive in some respects. For example, its massive backbone was solid. Later sauropods had hollow areas in their bones to reduce the weight.

Cetiosaurus

CHASMOSAURUS

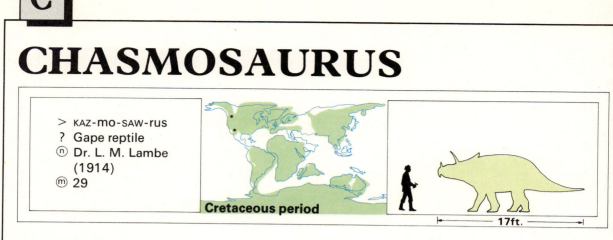

> KAZ-mo-SAW-rus
? Gape reptile
ⓝ Dr. L. M. Lambe (1914)
ⓜ 29

Cretaceous period

17ft.

Chasmosaurus was the earliest long-frilled ceratopsian. At the back of its head there was a long frill made from the skull bones which had grown backward. The frill was longer than the skull itself, and it had large holes in it to make it weigh less. The strong neck muscles that *Chasmosaurus* needed to hold up its heavy head would have been fixed to the frill. There were small horns over the eyes and one on the nose.

Two species of *Chasmosaurus* have been named from the Red Deer River region of Alberta, Canada. One has short blunt horns over its eyes while the other has long pointed horns. Otherwise, the two are very similar, and it has been suggested that these may be the male and female animals of a single species.

Chasmosaurus skull (5 feet wide).

CLAOSAURUS

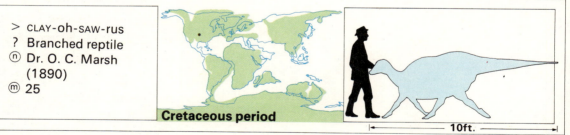

> CLAY-oh-SAW-rus
? Branched reptile
ⓝ Dr. O. C. Marsh (1890)
ⓜ 25

Cretaceous period

10ft.

Claosaurus was one of the earliest duck-billed dinosaurs. It hardly had any crest at all and it had primitive legs and feet.

The name *Claosaurus* was given by Othniel C. Marsh to a specimen which he had thought, in 1872, was a new species of *Hadrosaurus*. Later he realized that it was a new form. Marsh re-named *Claosaurus* in May 1890, but Edward Cope, his great enemy *(see pages 14–15)* had already given the name *Pteropelyx* to another similar duckbill in March 1890, and there was much argument about which name should be used!

COELOPHYSIS

> SEEL-oh-FY-sis
? Hollow form
(n) Dr. E. D. Cope (1889)
(m) 7, 20, 32, 49

Triassic period

12ft.

Coelophysis is the oldest well-known dinosaur. There are several Late Triassic dinosaurs of about the same age—such as *Ischisaurus, Procompsognathus, Saltopus,* and *Staurikosaurus*—but each of these is known from only one or two skeletons. In 1947, a mass of a hundred or more specimens of

Coelophysis

Coelophysis was found at Ghost Ranch, New Mexico. The specimens dug up there included young and old animals which ranged in size from 3 to 10 feet long. *Coelophysis* was very slim and it could have run either on two or four legs. The neck and tail were long. The hands had only three fingers, but they were strong. *Coelophysis* had a long narrow head, and its sharp, jagged teeth show that it ate meat—probably the small, lizard-like animals that were found with it.

Some of the skeletons were found with small *Coelophysis* bones inside. It was thought that these were babies, ready to be born. However, they are rather too big for that, and it may be that *Coelophysis* was a cannibal.

COELUROSAURIA

The infraorder Coelurosauria includes a variety of small and medium-sized meat-eating dinosaurs. Most of them ran upright on their hind legs, which were long and slender, and used their strong hands to catch prey and to carry food.

The Coelurosauria has been a difficult group to classify. This is because it includes some of the earliest and most primitive dinosaurs from the Late Triassic, such as *Coelophysis* and *Halticosaurus*, as well as some later forms from the Late Jurassic, such as *Coelurus* and *Compsognathus*.

These early forms are called the coelophysids, and they can be told apart from the later forms, the coelurids, mainly by the shape of their heads and hands. The coelophysids had large wedge-shaped heads and three or four claws on their hands. The coelurids had low heads and always three claws.

The Late Jurassic coelurids follow after a gap in the Early and Middle Jurassic for which no remains have been found. They are from North America *(Coelurus, Ornitholestes)* and Europe *(Compsognathus)*. Someday, scientists will find more species of coelurosaurs to fill the gap. A few poor remains tell us that the coelurosaurs probably lived on into the Cretaceous period, but they died out long before the end of the age of the dinosaurs.

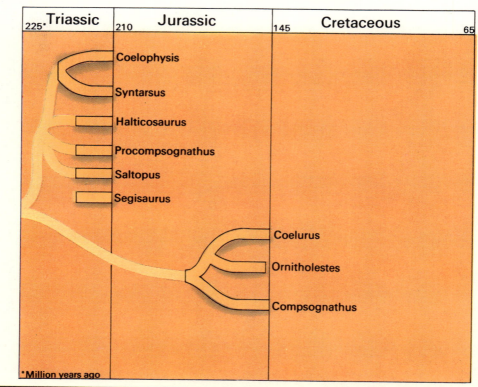

225*Triassic	210 Jurassic	145 Cretaceous 65

Coelophysis

Syntarsus

Halticosaurus

Procompsognathus

Saltopus

Segisaurus

Coelurus

Ornitholestes

Compsognathus

*Million years ago

Syntarsus

Ornitholestes

Procompsognathus

Compsognathus

Coelophysis

COELURUS

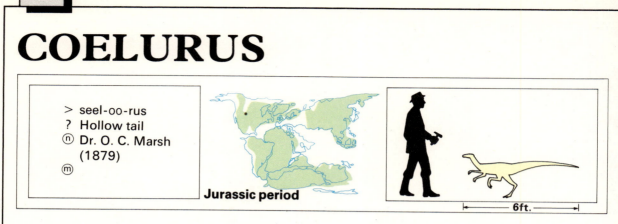

> seel-oo-rus
? Hollow tail
ⓝ Dr. O. C. Marsh (1879)
ⓜ

Jurassic period

6ft.

Coelurus was a small dinosaur—only 6 feet long and lightly built. Its skull would have fit in a human hand. Its bones were very light – the tail vertebrae were hollow. The hand had only three fingers: the thumb was short and the other two fingers were long with sharp curved claws.

The original specimen of *Coelurus* was a single bone from the backbone which was named *Coelurus fragilis* by Othniel C. Marsh in 1879. This poor specimen was forgotten until much later, after *Ornitholestes* was named in 1903. *Ornitholestes* was based on a nearly complete skeleton which came from the same part of Wyoming that had produced the single bone of *Coelurus*. Everyone assumed that

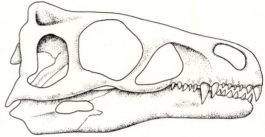

Coelurus skull (2 feet wide)

these two bones were from the same animal, and the names were combined. However, a much more recent study has shown that there really were two different small meat-eaters in the fossil bed called the "Morrison Formation" of Wyoming, living under the feet of *Allosaurus*, *Apatosaurus*, *Brachiosaurus*, *Ceratosaurus*, and *Stegosaurus*.

COMPSOGNATHUS

> KOMP-SOW-NAY-thus
? Pretty jaw
ⓝ Dr. J. A. Wagner (1859)
ⓜ 42, 51

Triassic period

2ft.

Compsognathus was closely related to Coelurus, and lived at about the same time, but in Europe. The adult was one of the smallest known dinosaurs. Compsognathus could reach up to 2 feet—more than half of this length being made up by the long, thin tail. A single skeleton was found in Germany in 1861. In this specimen, the tail is lifted up, and the head is bent back over the tail. This was thought to be an unnatural position showing that Compsognathus was in agony. However, it is a common feature of dead animals that the head bends back as the neck muscles dry out. This specimen, like some of those of Coelophysis, had small bones inside it, and it was thought that Compsognathus was also a cannibal. It has now been shown that the bones belonged to a lizard. Another good specimen of Compsognathus was found more recently in southern France, and it is larger than the original German one.

A herd of Compsognathus

CORYTHOSAURUS

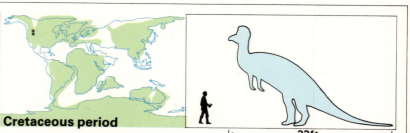

> ko-RITH-oh-SAW-rus
? Helmeted reptile
(n) Dr. B. Brown (1914)
(m) 6, 7, 9, 16, 29, 32

Cretaceous period

33ft.

Corythosaurus is one of the best-known of the hadrosaurs (duck-billed dinosaurs). It was a large animal—over 33 feet long. The crest on top of the head was high and narrow, shaped rather like half a dinner plate set up on edge. The nasal tubes ran from the nostrils on the snout up into the crest and then down again into the mouth. *Corythosaurus* may have used this complicated breathing system to make loud bellows and honks.

There are several species of *Corythosaurus* which have different shapes of crest. Even within a single species of *Corythosaurus*, the crest on the skull could vary a great deal. In very young animals there was almost no crest at all—just a small bulge on the forehead. In slightly older ones, the crest grew out a little more in front of the eyes. Finally, it grew back and upward as a tall ridge that started in front of the eyes and ran to the very back of the skull. This crest was formed from the nasal bones—bones which in most dinosaurs covered the top of the snout. Two species of *Corythosaurus*, *C. casuarius* and *C. intermedius* are told apart by the different size of the crest. It has now

been suggested that these might both belong to the same species, with the males having a larger crest.

Corythosaurus

DACENTRURUS

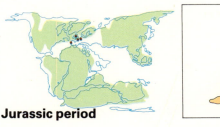

> DA-sen-TROO-rus
? Pointed tail
Ⓝ Sir Richard Owen (1875)
Ⓜ 59

Jurassic period

size unknown

Dacentrurus was one of the earliest stegosaurs but it is known only from odd bones found in England, France, and Portugal. *Dacentrurus* had paired spines on its back, but probably no plates. Some of the specimens show close similarities to *Stegosaurus*.

The first bones of *Dacentrurus* were found in England in the 1870s. Indeed, these were the first remains of a stegosaur to be found anywhere

in the world. The armor plates and spikes showed that a new dinosaur group had been discovered. They were described by Sir Richard Owen in 1875, and named *Omosaurus armatus* at first. They were later named *Dacentrurus* since the name *Omosaurus* had already been given by Joseph Leidy in 1856 to a different animal.

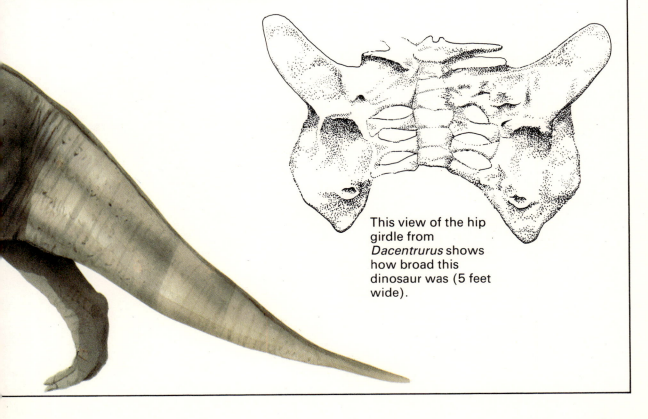

This view of the hip girdle from *Dacentrurus* shows how broad this dinosaur was (5 feet wide).

DASPLETOSAURUS

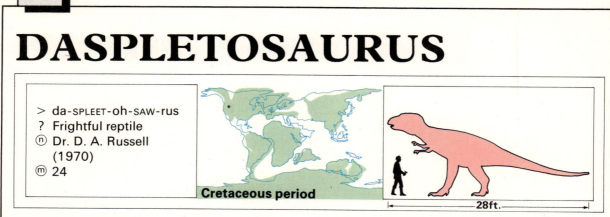

> da-SPLEET-oh-SAW-rus
? Frightful reptile
ⓝ Dr. D. A. Russell (1970)
ⓜ 24

Cretaceous period

28ft.

Daspletosaurus was a fearsome meat-eater, 28 feet long. It had a huge head, deep jaws and dagger-like teeth. Its powerful hind legs each had three toes, but the arms were weak and had only two fingers each. *Daspletosaurus* could have attacked and eaten the duck-billed dinosaurs or ceratopsians that lived with it.

The first nearly-complete skeleton of *Daspletosaurus* was found in 1921 in the famous Red Deer River area of Alberta, Canada. At first, this was identified as *Gorgosaurus* (another name for *Albertosaurus*). However, more detailed study revealed that this was a different animal, being more heavily built than *Albertosaurus*, and having a larger fore limb than its other tyrannosaurid relatives. *Daspletosaurus* and *Albertosaurus* lived together at the same time in Alberta, and it seems likely that *Daspletosaurus* fed on heavier prey than the lighter *Albertosaurus*.

Daspletosaurus

DATOUSAURUS

> DAT-OO-SAW-rus
? Datou (where found) reptile
(n) Prof. Dong Zhiming & Dr. Tang Zilu (1984)
(m)

Jurassic period

46ft.

Datousaurus is one of the oldest known sauropods, dating from about the same time as *Barapasaurus* and *Cetiosaurus*. It was found in dinosaur beds in Sichuan Province by Chinese expeditions in 1979–81, together with another new form of sauropod, *Shunosaurus*. *Datousaurus* had a big skull with many large, spoon-shaped teeth. Its neck was shorter than in many later sauropods and it had strong limbs. These new discoveries from China show that the large sauropods, which developed in the Middle Jurassic period, spread rapidly all over the world from places as far apart as England, Argentina, India, Australia and China.

DEINOCHEIRUS

> DINE-oh-KIRE-us
? Terrible hand
(n) Drs. H. Osmólska & E. Roniewicz (1967)
(m) 50

Cretaceous period

40ft.

Deinocheirus is one of the most amazing dinosaur fossils known. It is a pair of huge arms and nothing else. The arms were found on a recent expedition to southern Mongolia by a joint Polish-Mongolian team. Each arm is 8 feet long. Each hand has only three fingers, and these all have powerful claws. The claws themselves are each about 10 inches long. If the arms belonged to a meat-eating dinosaur of a normal shape, it would have been unbelievably huge. We cannot even guess what the whole animal looked like. The large claws might suggest that *Deinocheirus* was a deinonychosaur. However, the very long, thin arms are more like those of an ornithomimosaur in shape. The three slender fingers are also a feature of ornithomimosaurs. Until more bones are found, no one can say for sure what type of dinosaur *Deinocheirus* really is.

DEINONYCHOSAURIA

One of the most exciting groups of dinosaurs, the infraorder Deinonychosauria, has only recently been studied in detail. Specimens of deinonychosaurs, such as *Dromaeosaurus* and *Velociraptor*, have been known for many years, but it was the discovery of *Deinonychus* which alerted paleontologists to the fact that this was a major new group.

The deinonychosaurs include some of the most remarkable and fearsome meat-eating dinosaurs. They were all armed with massive pointed claws, shaped like great scythes, on their feet and often also on their hands. These claws were 12 inches long, and were used by the deinonychosaurs to slash at their prey.

There were at least two families of deinonychosaurs, the dromaeosaurids and the saurornithoidids. The Dromaeosauridae includes the claw-slashers from the Middle and Late Cretaceous of North America (*Deinonychus, Dromaeosaurus*) and Asia (*Hulsanpes, Velociraptor*). These were all medium-sized, agile animals with one major slashing claw on the second toe of each foot. The Saurornithoididae dates from the Late Cretaceous of North America (*Troodon*) and Asia (*Saurornithoides*). These were lighter and slimmer than the dromaeosaurids; their slashing claws were not so massive and their heads were narrower.

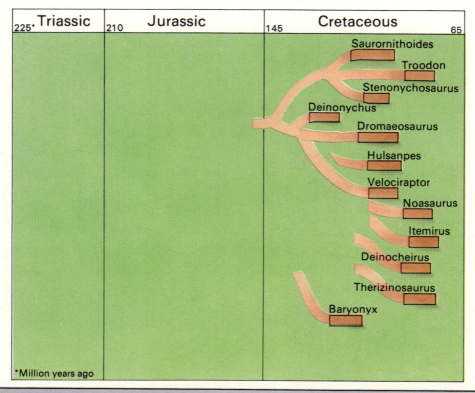

225* Triassic	210 Jurassic	145 Cretaceous 65
		Saurornithoides
		Troodon
		Stenonychosaurus
		Deinonychus
		Dromaeosaurus
		Hulsanpes
		Velociraptor
		Noasaurus
		Itemirus
		Deinocheirus
		Therizinosaurus
		Baryonyx

*Million years ago

Deinonychus

Velociraptor

Stenonychosaurus

DEINONYCHUS

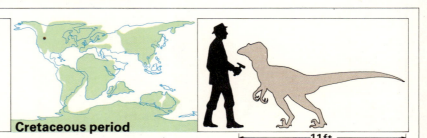

> DIE-no-NIKE-us
? Terrible claw
ⓝ Dr. J. H. Ostrom (1969)
ⓜ 6, 25

Cretaceous period

11ft.

Deinonychus was one of the most exciting dinosaurs to be discovered in the 1960s. It was represented by several well-preserved skeletons from a site in southern Montana, from which detailed restorations were done. *Deinonychus* was 10 to 13 feet long—larger than its relatives, *Dromaeosaurus* and *Velociraptor*. It had a lightly built skull, and its jaws were armed with large backward-curving, flesh-eating teeth. *Deinonychus* had strong, grasping fingers on its hands. Each of the three fingers on each hand was armed with

It would have balanced on one foot in order to swing the claw to open the belly of its prey. Its tail was stiffened by long rods of bone.

Deinonychus

a heavy claw, and there were powerful muscles to allow it to slash at its prey. Its most remarkable feature, however, was the large, curved, scythe-like claw on the second toe of the foot. The other toes had shorter claws. When *Deinonychus* ran, it flicked the big claw back and placed the shorter toes on the ground. *Deinonychus* used its big claw to attack other dinosaurs.

DICRAEOSAURUS

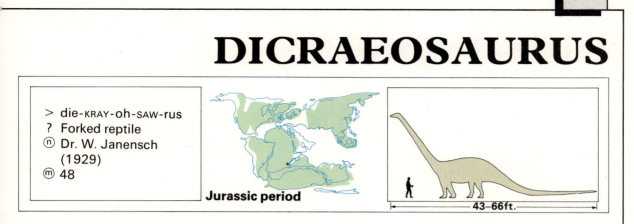

> die-KRAY-oh-SAW-rus
? Forked reptile
ⓝ Dr. W. Janensch (1929)
ⓜ 48

Jurassic period

43–66ft.

Dicraeosaurus is known from a nearly-complete skeleton, and it appears to be related to *Apatosaurus* and *Diplodocus*. The name "forked reptile" refers to a strange feature of the vertebrae of the backbone. The spine on top of each vertebra is split in two and form a shape like a letter Y. The skull is long and sloping with a range of long peg-like teeth at the front of the upper and lower jaws. The openings of the nostrils and eye sockets are smaller than in many of its relatives.

DILOPHOSAURUS

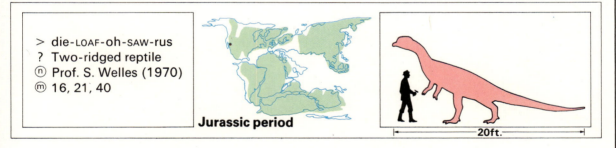

> die-LOAF-oh-SAW-rus
? Two-ridged reptile
ⓝ Prof. S. Welles (1970)
ⓜ 16, 21, 40

Jurassic period

20ft.

Dilophosaurus is the oldest well-known, large, meat-eating dinosaur. The most amazing thing about *Dilophosaurus* is that it had two very thin ridges on top of its skull. These were shaped like a pair of half dinner plates set up on edge and side by side. *Dilophosaurus* had sharp fangs, but its jaws seem to have been weaker than those of its later relatives, and it may be that *Dilophosaurus* was a scavenger, feeding on dead animals rather than actively killing its own prey.

DIPLODOCUS

> dip-LOD-oh-kus
? Double beam
ⓝ Dr. O. C. Marsh (1878)
ⓜ 7, 9, 10, 11, 13, 15, 18,
   23, 30, 45, 51, 57, 63

Jurassic period

88ft.

Diplodocus was 88 feet long, but it weighed only 10 to 11 tons, much less than many of its relatives. Most of its length was made up from the long, thin neck and whip-like tail. The name "double beam" describes a special feature of the backbone. There were small bones below the backbone which had a piece running forward as well as the normal piece running back—a "double beam." There were small claws on the inner toes of the feet, and these may have been used to fight off meat-eaters. Many skeletons of *Diplodocus* were collected in western America around 1900. The Scottish-American millionaire Andrew Carnegie paid for much of the collecting, and the best skeleton was called *Diplodocus carnegiei*.

Diplodocus

DRAVIDOSAURUS

> dra-VID-oh-SAW-rus
? Reptile from southern India
(n) P. Yadagiri & K. Ayyasami (1979)
(m)

Jurassic period

10ft.

Dravidosaurus is the last known stegosaur. Most stegosaurs, like *Stegosaurus* and *Kentrosaurus*, come from the Late Jurassic, so that there is a span of millions of years between these and *Dravidosaurus*. *Dravidosaurus* had an armor of plates on its back, and strange spines which bulged halfway up. It was named in 1979 from an incomplete skull, but other specimens have since been found. It is strange that *Dravidosaurus* is not only the last stegosaur, but also the only one that ever lived in India, as far as we know.

DROMAEOSAURUS

> DROME-ee-oh-SAW-rus
? Running reptile
(n) Drs. W. D. Matthew & B. Brown (1922)
(m) 32

Cretaceous period

6ft.

Dromaeosaurus was a small active dinosaur. It was like *Deinonychus* in that it had a special sharp claw on its foot for attacking other dinosaurs. *Dromaeosaurus* was smaller than *Deinonychus*, and it could have just looked a ten-year-old in the eye if it stood up straight.

When the first specimen of *Dromaeosaurus* was collected beside the Red Deer River, Canada, in 1914,

Dromaeosaurus skull (7 inches wide).

it was not clear what sort of dinosaur it was. Some people thought it was a tiny carnosaur (a relative of *Tyrannosaurus!*) while others thought it was related to *Compsognathus*.

DRYOSAURUS

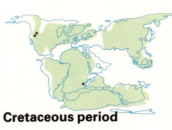

> DRY-oh-SAW-rus
? Oak reptile
(n) Dr. O. C. Marsh (1894)
(m) 9, 11, 48

Cretaceous period

10–13ft.

Dryosaurus was a relative of *Hypsilophodon*, but much larger: *Dryosaurus* was 10 to 13 feet long. It had long, powerful legs and strong arms each with five fingers, but it had only three toes on its foot, while *Hypsilophodon* had four. *Dryosaurus* could have run fast on its hind legs and its tail was stiff and could have been used for balance. It probably used its hands to gather plants to eat. It had sharp, ridged cheek teeth. There is also evidence that

Dryosaurus had fleshy cheeks where it could store its food while chewing it properly.

Dryosaurus had large eyes, with a special bone in the upper part to support the eyeball and the skin around the eye. It is known from several skeletons and skulls from Africa and North America, which proves that these two parts of the world were connected 140 million years ago. *Dryosaurus* lived with the well-known sauropods *Apatosaurus*, *Brachiosaurus*, and *Diplodocus*, the stegosaurs *Stegosaurus* and *Kentrosaurus*, and the meat-eaters *Allosaurus*, *Coelurus*, and *Elaphrosaurus*.

Dryosaurus

DRYPTOSAURUS

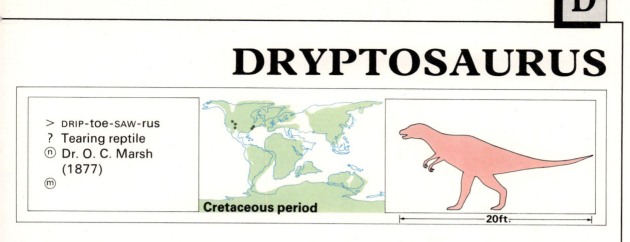

> DRIP-toe-SAW-rus
? Tearing reptile
Ⓝ Dr. O. C. Marsh (1877)
Ⓜ

Cretaceous period

20ft.

Dryptosaurus was a meat eater that was found all over North America. Many discoveries of odd teeth and jaw bones have been named as *Dryptosaurus*—at least 12 species have been described, and yet no one really knows what it looked like. The only skeleton was collected in 1866 and named *Laelaps* by E.D. Cope, one of the famous dinosaur collectors of the North American "bone wars" *(see pages 14–15)*. The name *Laelaps* was based on the name for a hunting dog from the ancient Greek myths, and Cope had a model made that showed *Laelaps* leaping through the air to attack another dinosaur. Unfortunately, we cannot use the name *Laelaps* because an insect had been given that name before.

DYOPLOSAURUS

> die-o-plo-SAW-rus
? Doubly armoured reptile
Ⓝ Dr. W. Parks (1924)
Ⓜ

Cretaceous period

20ft.

Dyoplosaurus was a large ankylosaur which was closely related to *Euoplocephalus*. Fossils of this dinosaur were found at the beginning of this century on the Red Deer River in Alberta, Canada, together with remains of *Euoplocephalus*. Some scientists believe that *Dyoplosaurus* may be the same as *Euoplocephalus*.

Dyoplosaurus had massive legs, and it was over 20 feet long. The last ten bones of the tail were joined together by fused bone and strengthened tendons. At the very end was a great lump of bone made from four joined blocks which formed a club. The whole solid club was 4 feet long and very heavy. It must have been a useful weapon against *Tyrannosaurus*.

EDMONTOSAURUS

> ed-MONT-oh-SAW-rus
? Edmonton reptile
ⓝ Dr. L. M. Lambe
(1917)
ⓜ 16, 29, 30

Cretaceous period

33–42ft.

Edmontosaurus was a flat-headed, duck-billed dinosaur, rather like *Anatosaurus* and *Shantungosaurus*. *Edmontosaurus* is quite well known because several skeletons have been found. It was one of the largest duckbills, at up to 42 feet long. It could walk on all fours or on its hind legs alone. There were small hooves on the toes and on two of the fingers. The skull was low in front and high at the back with a wide, duck-like beak (as in *Anatosaurus*). *Edmontosaurus* did not have a crest, unlike many duckbills. However, there might have been an area of loose skin on top of the snout which could have been blown up like a balloon to make a loud bellowing call.

Edmontosaurus had about 1,000 strong teeth, and probably fed on tough plants that needed to be well chopped up before swallowing.

Edmontosaurus

ELAPHROSAURUS

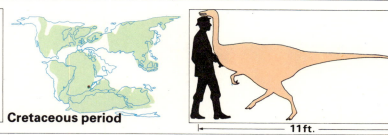

> ee-LAF-roe-SAW-rus
? Light reptile
ⓝ Dr. W. Janensch
(1920)
ⓜ 48

Cretaceous period

11ft.

Elaphrosaurus is probably the oldest known ornithomimosaur: all the others, like *Ornithomimus* and *Struthiomimus*, lived in the Late Cretaceous, 70 million years later. It is not certain that *Elaphrosaurus* really was an ornithomimosaur because of this great gap of time, but it had many of this group's characteristics.

Elaphrosaurus was 11 feet long, and not as ostrich-like as its later relatives. It had long, slender legs and was obviously a fast runner. Its arms were short. Both the feet and hands had only three fingers or toes.

Elaphrosaurus is best known from the famous Tendaguru dinosaur beds in Tanzania, where a headless skeleton was found earlier this century. If a skull of *Elaphrosaurus* is ever discovered, it will be possible to decide whether it lacked teeth, like the ornithomimosaurs, or not. The Tendaguru beds have also yielded the dinosaurs *Barosaurus*, *Brachiosaurus*, and *Kentrosaurus*.

Elaphrosaurus

EUHELOPUS

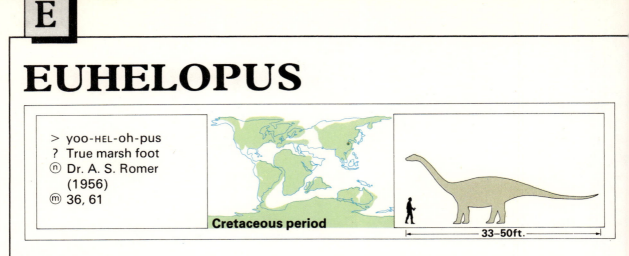

> yoo-HEL-oh-pus
? True marsh foot
(n) Dr. A. S. Romer (1956)
(m) 36, 61

Cretaceous period

33–50ft.

Euhelopus was a large sauropod related to *Camarasaurus* and *Opisthocoelicaudia*. It may have been 33 to 50 feet long. It had a long neck and head, and the front legs were longer than the hind legs. The back sloped, as in *Camarasaurus*.

This was one of the first dinosaurs from China to be described. It was collected in the 1920s by a Swedish expedition. A sauropod specimen collected in the 1970s by Chinese scientists in Upper Jurassic sediments, and named *Omeisaurus*, may actually belong to *Euhelopus*. This specimen has a strange wedge-shaped skull with nostrils very near the front of the skull, instead of set back as in most other sauropods.

EUSKELOSAURUS

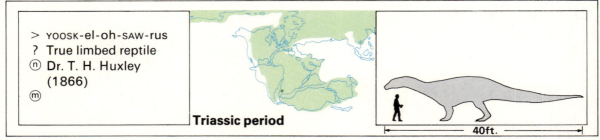

> yoosk-el-oh-saw-rus
? True limbed reptile
(n) Dr. T. H. Huxley (1866)
(m)

Triassic period

40ft.

Euskelosaurus was one of the first dinosaurs to be discovered and recorded from Africa. A small set of leg bones was sent to England from South Africa and named *Euskelosaurus* in 1866. Since then, many more specimens of this animal have been found. The bones are huge: the thigh bone alone is 3 feet long. Unfortunately, there is no skull of *Euskelosaurus* yet known, but the neck was probably long and the head small, similar to other prosauropods. Because only a few fairly poor fossils have been found, it is not certain exactly to which dinosaurs *Euskelosaurus* was related. It was a prosauropod, and it may have been related to either *Plateosaurus* or *Melanorosaurus*.

FABROSAURUS

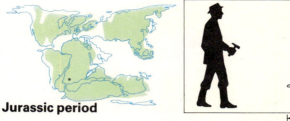

> FAB-roe-SAW-rus
? Fabre's reptile
ⓝ Dr. L. Ginsberg
  (1964)
ⓜ

Jurassic period

|← 3ft. →|

Fabrosaurus was an early primitive ornithopod, related to *Scutellosaurus*. It was only 3 feet long, and would not have been able to look over your dinner table at home if it had stood up as straight as it could. *Fabrosaurus* was very lightly built, and it ran on its hind legs. It had strong arms and hands. The teeth were strong, and they had frilled or knobby edges. This shows that *Fabrosaurus* could use its teeth to chop up tough vegetation.

The original specimen of *Fabrosaurus*, found in 1964, was only a broken piece of jaw with a few teeth in place. A more complete skeleton was found later which could well be *Fabrosaurus*, but it has been named as a new genus, *Lesothosaurus*.

Fabrosaurus

GALLIMIMUS

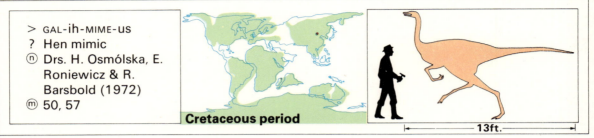

> GAL-ih-MIME-us
? Hen mimic
(n) Drs. H. Osmólska, E. Roniewicz & R. Barsbold (1972)
(m) 50, 57

Cretaceous period

13ft.

Gallimimus was probably the largest ornithomimosaur, and it is known from three fairly complete skeletons. It was about 13 feet long, slightly bigger than its close relatives *Ornithomimus* and *Struthiomimus*. *Gallimimus* had hands that could not grasp things, and so probably could not have torn meat up. It has been suggested that it scraped at the soil and may have fed on eggs. *Gallimimus* had a long snout with a broad, flat end, large eyes, and long, toothless jaws.

Gallimimus

GERANOSAURUS

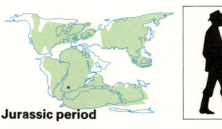

> jer-AN-oh-SAW-rus
? Crane reptile
ⓝ Dr. R. Broom
ⓜ

Jurassic period

4ft.

Geranosaurus was a small ornithopod that was closely related to *Heterodontosaurus* and *Lycorhinus*. It is known only from parts of its jaws and a few other bones which were found early this century. It was the first known representative of its group. The jaws show that it had sharp teeth at the front of the jaw, a pair of fangs behind, and ridged

cheek teeth at the back. The front teeth were used to snip pieces off plants.

Since that first find, six or more heterodontosaurids have been named from South Africa. Some have a pair of long, tusk-like teeth on the upper and lower jaws, while others lack these tusks. These could be males and females of the same species.

GOYOCEPHALE

> GOY-oh-KEF-a-lee
? Decorated head
ⓝ Drs. A. Perle, T. Maryańska & H. Osmólska (1982)
ⓜ

Cretaceous period

6ft.

Goyocephale is known from partial remains of the skull and skeleton, including much of the tail, and fore and hind limbs.

Goyocephale is apparently related to the low-domed *Homalocephale*: both were small animals, being only 2 to 5 feet in total body length. The thickened skull roof bones of *Goyocephale* were covered with a

rough pattern of pits and knobs, and there were four or five broad spines low down at the back of the head. The hip girdle in *Goyocephale* was broad, and it was attached to the backbone very firmly. This may have been to withstand the shocks of head-butting which would have been felt from the top of the head, down the backbone, to the legs.

HADROSAURUS

> HAD-roe-SAW-rus
? Big reptile
ⓝ Prof. J. Leidy (1858)
ⓜ 6, 29, 32

Cretaceous period

26–33ft.

Hadrosaurus was the first dinosaur skeleton to be named in North America. A skeleton without the skull was collected from New Jersey and called *Hadrosaurus* in 1858. It had the fore limbs and hind limbs preserved, and it was, at that time, the most complete dinosaur skeleton found anywhere in the world. This find allowed Joseph Leidy, the first North American dinosaur expert, to make a lifelike restoration of *Hadrosaurus*. Until 1858, everyone had thought that all dinosaurs walked on all fours, but Leidy could see that *Hadrosaurus* stood on its hind legs. He believed that it squatted like a kangaroo— which was not quite right, but it was the best dinosaur reconstruction of the time.

When a skull was discovered it was long and low with a typical "duck-billed" shape, like *Anatosaurus* and *Edmontosaurus*. There was a rounded hump in front of the eyes and above the nostrils.

Hadrosaurus

HALTICOSAURUS

> hal-TIK-oh-SAW-rus
? Nimble reptile
ⓝ Prof. F. von Huene (1908)
ⓜ 64

Triassic period

18ft.

Halticosaurus was a large coelurosaur, up to 18 feet long. It had five fingers on its hand, a feature of primitive dinosaurs. The arms were short, and the legs were strong. The head was long and large. In the drawing of the skull you can see the pointed meat-eating teeth, and the light construction, with lots of holes. From the front, the holes are the nostril, an opening of unknown function, the eye socket, and jaw-muscle openings. Two skeletons and a skull of *Halticosaurus* have been found in Germany, together with the larger prosauropod *Plateosaurus*.

Halticosaurus skull (1½ feet wide).

HETERODONTOSAURUS

> HET-er-oh-DONT-oh-
SAW-rus
? Reptile with different
teeth
ⓝ Drs. A. W. Crompton
& A. J. Charig (1962)
ⓜ 5, 19

Jurassic period

← 4ft. →

Heterodontosaurus is the best-known early ornithopod. It had three different kinds of teeth: sharp teeth at the front, fangs, and broad-ridged cheek teeth. The front teeth were used for cutting off pieces of leaves, the sharp fangs for puncturing tough stems, and the broad cheek teeth for grinding up the food. Some specimens had no fangs or tusks; these may have been females. This kind of tooth arrangement is unusual for a dinosaur because most dinosaurs had only one kind of tooth.

Heterodontosaurus was about 4 feet long, and it was an active animal that could run on its hind legs. The backbone was strengthened with slender rods of bone along the sides. These would have allowed *Heterodontosaurus* to hold its tail out straight when it wanted to run fast.

HOMALOCEPHALE

> hom-AL-oh-KEF-al-ee
? Level head
ⓝ Drs. T. Maryańska &
H. Osmólska (1974)
ⓜ 50

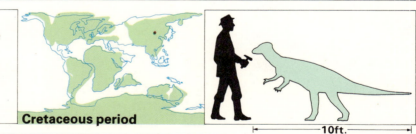

Cretaceous period

← 10ft. →

Homalocephale was a medium-sized pachycephalosaur with a flat head. The top of its skull was very thick with a rough surface covered with pits and bony knobs. The most important feature of *Homalocephale* is that much of the skeleton has been discovered. Many pachycephalosaurs are known only from the thickened skull roofs, and nothing is known of other parts of the body. In *Homalocephale*, the hip bones are very wide and are loosely attached to as many as eight vertebrae of the backbone. It has been suggested that *Homalocephale* may have given birth to live young, rather than laying eggs, because of the breadth of its hip region.

HYLAEOSAURUS

> HY-lee-oh-SAW-rus
? Woodland reptile
ⓝ Dr. G. A. Mantell
  (1833)
ⓜ

Cretaceous period

18ft.

Hylaeosaurus is the oldest, fairly well-known ankylosaur. Older ankylosaurs have been reported from the Middle and Late Jurassic of England, but they are known only from odd armor plates and spines. *Hylaeosaurus* is known from partial skeletons, but its armor is more often found.

Hylaeosaurus was about 18 feet long. It had an armor of spines that stuck out sideways and upward along the back and tail. The top of the head was thick and bony. It was only the third dinosaur to be named, after *Megalosaurus* and *Iguanodon*. A skeleton from Sussex, southeast England, was named as *Hylaeosaurus* in 1833 by Dr. Gideon Mantell, who

had also named the first *Iguanodon*. The name "woodland reptile" refers to the fact that the fossil came from the Tilgate Forest in Sussex. Unfortunately, only the front half of the skeleton was found, and it is still embedded in a block of limestone in the British Museum. This means that the legs and the body armor have had to be guessed at in the reconstruction drawing. Information for this has come from *Polacanthus*, also from the Early Cretaceous of southern England, which is clearly a close relative. Indeed, some scientists have suggested that they might both be the same kind of animal.

Hylaeosaurus

HYPACROSAURUS

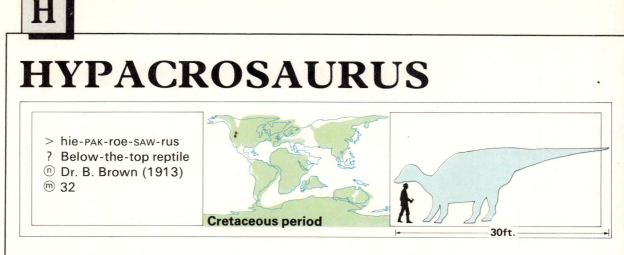

> hie-PAK-roe-SAW-rus
? Below-the-top reptile
ⓝ Dr. B. Brown (1913)
ⓜ 32

Cretaceous period

30ft.

Hypacrosaurus was a large, duck-billed dinosaur, about 30 feet long. It had a short, high skull and its crest

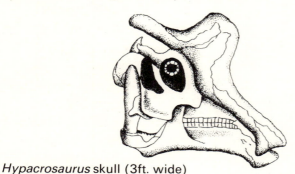

Hypacrosaurus skull (3ft. wide)

was rounded, but lower and fatter than that of *Corythosaurus*. The crest ran out backward into a solid bony spike. If you look at the drawing of the skull, you can see that the crest is built up from the bones at the front of the skull. These have grown up and backward. *Hypacrosaurus* had dozens of strong teeth which formed a large area for grinding and chopping tough plant food. As the teeth wore down they were replaced by new ones.

HYPSELOSAURUS

> HIP-sel-oh-SAW-rus
? High-ridged reptile
ⓝ Dr P. Matheron
(1869)
ⓜ 54

Cretaceous period

40ft.

Hypselosaurus was a medium-sized sauropod. The most interesting thing about it is that its bones have been found together with large eggs and pieces of eggshell in the south of France. The eggs are big—about 12 inches long and 10 inches across; bigger than a football. Of course, for a

40-foot dinosaur, a 12-inch egg is not very large but it is about as big an egg as could possibly exist. This is because the size is limited by the thickness of the shell. As an egg gets bigger, the shell has to get thicker. But the eggshell had to be thin enough to allow the baby to break out.

HYPSILOPHODON

> hip-see-LOAF-oh-don
? High-ridged tooth
ⓝ Prof. T. H. Huxley (1870)
ⓜ 46, 49, 56, 57

Cretaceous period

6ft.

Hypsilophodon was an interesting, medium-sized ornithopod. It was 5 to 7 feet long. It had short arms, each with five fingers, and long legs, each with four toes. *Hypsilophodon* could run fast, and it had a long, stiff tail which it used for balance. It was once thought that *Hypsilophodon* climbed trees, but this is unlikely since it could not grasp the branches. *Hypsilophodon* had no teeth at the front of its mouth, but only a bony beak—possibly covered with horn, and a row of short chopping teeth farther back. It could have nipped plants off with its beak, and chopped them up with its cheek teeth.

The overall shape of the head is very like that of a sheep or goat, and it seems that *Hypsilophodon* was as common as these animals in the Early Cretaceous forests of the south of England. The first skeleton of *Hypsilophodon* was found in 1849, and others in 1868 by the Reverend William Fox, a noted local collector. At first, the scientists thought these were young *Iguanodon*, and it was only a few years later that T. H. Huxley realized that they represented a new form of dinosaur.

Hypsilophodon

IGUANODON

> ig-WA-no-don
? Iguana tooth
ⓝ Dr. G. A. Mantell (1825)
ⓜ 43, 46, 47, 51, 52, 56, 57, 59, 60, 62, 63

Cretaceous period

30ft.

Iguanodon was the second dinosaur to be named—in 1825. *Iguanodon* was up to 30 feet long and stood 16 feet high—about the height of a second story window. It had strong hind limbs with three big toes, each with a hoof-like nail. The hand had four long fingers and a pointed spike-like thumb, which was probably used as a weapon. The tail was flattened and stiff, and *Iguanodon* could have run well on its hind legs or walked on all fours. This is shown by the presence of small hooves on three fingers of the hand. There were no teeth at the front of the jaw—only a bony beak like that of *Hypsilophodon*. The cheek teeth were strong and ridged. *Iguanodon* may have pulled plants into its mouth with its tongue, and nipped them off with its beak.

Iguanodon was a very widespread dinosaur. Hundreds of skeletons have been found in Lower Cretaceous rocks in the south of England, in Belgium, Germany and possibly also in north Africa and the United States.

Iguanodon tooth (2 inches long).

Iguanodon

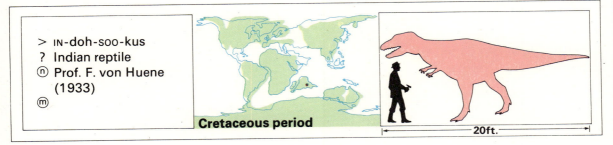

INDOSUCHUS

> IN-doh-soo-kus
? Indian reptile
ⓝ Prof. F. von Huene (1933)
ⓜ

Cretaceous period

20ft.

The Indian tyrannosaurid *Indosuchus* is known from only a few remains, and its relation to other dinosaurs is not entirely certain, although it shows a resemblance to *Tyrannosaurus* and *Albertosaurus*. Specimens were collected on two expeditions, one led by Dr. Charles Matley of the Indian Geological Survey in 1917–19, and one by Barnum Brown of the American Museum of Natural History. The specimens consist of fragments of a skull, showing the teeth particularly well, and part of a skull roof. The teeth are up to 4 inches long—vicious and sharp, with zig-zag edges, just like a steak knife.

One of the jaw specimens has been X-rayed, and this shows how the teeth were replaced. Dinosaurs kept losing teeth, and large meat-eaters may have lost several teeth every time they attacked another dinosaur. However, unlike humans, dinosaurs had teeth growing continuously, and in the X-ray small teeth can be seen deep within the jaw bone and ready to move into place when others fall out. Humans have only two sets of teeth,

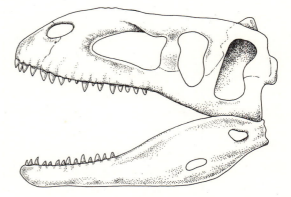

Indosuchus skull (30 inches wide)

the "milk" teeth that are lost when you are aged about six to ten, and the adult set. The giant meat-eating dinosaurs had new teeth all of the time, and they did not have to repair their old teeth, as we have to do.

ISCHISAURUS

> ISK-ih-SAW-rus
? Ischigualasto (where found) reptile
ⓝ Dr. O. A. Reig (1963)
ⓜ

Triassic period

6ft.

Ischisaurus was one of the first dinosaurs to be discovered, but only two specimens are known, and these include parts of the skull and legs. *Ischisaurus* was a medium-sized animal, 6 feet or so long. The arms were short and the hind legs rather longer, which suggests that *Ischisaurus* may have run on its hind legs. It has been suggested that *Ischisaurus* was the first ornithischian dinosaur, an ancestor of *Fabrosaurus* and *Heterodontosaurus*. However, more recent studies do not support this idea. *Ischisaurus* may be ancestral to most later dinosaurs, not just the ornithischians.

ITEMIRUS

> EAT-em-EE-rus
? Itemir (where found)
ⓝ Dr. S. M. Kurzanov (1976)
ⓜ

Cretaceous period

size unknown

Itemirus was a lightly built, agile meat-eating dinosaur but it is very poorly known. It was named from a small braincase in 1976. The shape of the braincase gives an idea of the shape that the brain would have been inside. This has suggested to the discoverers that *Itemirus* had a very good sense of sight, with large eyes, and good balance because those areas of the brain seem to have been well-developed.

Itemirus was considered to be so different from all other dinosaurs that its classifiers said that it belonged to a completely new group, the itemirids. However, more remains of the skull and skeleton would help to check whether this is correct or not.

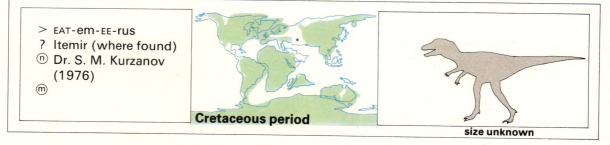

KENTROSAURUS

> KEN-tro-SAW-rus
? Pointed reptile
ⓝ Dr. E. Hennig (1915)
ⓜ 48, 49

Jurassic period

16ft.

Kentrosaurus was a large 16-foot-long plated dinosaur. Some good skeletons were collected at the famous Tendaguru site in Tanzania during the German-led excavations between 1909 and 1912, and these were sent to the Humboldt Museum in East Berlin. Many of these skeletons can no longer be seen there, and it is likely that they were destroyed by bombing during World War II.

Kentrosaurus was rather like *Stegosaurus* which lived in North America at the same time, except that *Kentrosaurus* had more primitive armor like that of *Lexovisaurus*. *Kentrosaurus* had small, flat, triangular plates on the neck and shoulders, and pairs of long spines on the back and tail. There was also a long spine over each hip which stuck out sideways and slightly downward. Unfortunately, very little is known of the skull, but the head seems to have been like that of *Stegosaurus*.

Kentrosaurus

LAMBEOSAURUS

> LAM-bee-oh-SAW-rus
? Lambe's (Canadian paleontologist) reptile
(n) Dr. W. Parks (1923)
(m) 7, 13, 27, 29, 32

Cretaceous period

50ft.

Lambeosaurus was a crested, duck-billed dinosaur related to *Corythosaurus* and *Hypacrosaurus*. *Lambeosaurus* had a square-shaped crest which pointed forward, with a long spine running backward. Some specimens have a larger crest than others, and these were originally thought to be two different species. It now seems that these may be males and females. The nostrils ran up from the snout and through the crest, so that the whole thing was hollow. In some specimens of *Lambeosaurus*, the crest is bigger than the skull. *Lambeosaurus* was big—about 50 feet long—and its bones are massive.

Lambeosaurus

Lambeosaurus skull (6 feet wide).

LEPTOCERATOPS

> LEP-toe-SER-a-tops
? Slim-horned face
ⓝ Dr. B. Brown (1914)
ⓜ 24

Cretaceous period

6–9ft.

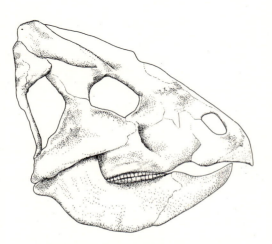

Leptoceratops skull (12 inches wide).

Leptoceratops was a small, horned dinosaur related to *Bagaceratops* and *Protoceratops*. It had short arms and long hind legs, so it could probably have run upright. The arms had small grasping hands that might have been used for gathering plant food, or carrying it. The skull was low and it had no trace of horns at all, unlike its relatives. *Leptoceratops* had a small frill at the back of its skull, and it is clearly a primitive form. There were no openings through the bone of the frill as in other ceratopsians. These apparently primitive characteristics are very unusual in view of the fact that *Leptoceratops* lived long after the origin of the ceratopsians. It seems that *Leptoceratops* kept its active habits, running upright on its hind limbs like the first ceratopsian, *Psittacosaurus*, even after all the other ceratopsians had changed to walking on all fours. *Leptoceratops* was 6 to 9 feet long.

LEXOVISAURUS

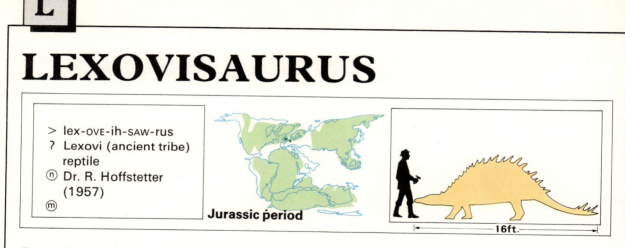

> lex-OVE-ih-SAW-rus
? Lexovi (ancient tribe) reptile
ⓝ Dr. R. Hoffstetter (1957)
ⓜ

Jurassic period

16ft.

Lexovisaurus was one of the first stegosaurs to be discovered. We know about it from pieces of armor and limb bones found in England and northern France. The French specimens show that *Lexovisaurus* was probably rather like *Kentrosaurus*. Its armor was a selection of flat plates and round, pointed spines that ran along the back and tail. There was a pair of long spines over the hips. *Lexovisaurus* was probably about 16 feet long.

Lexovisaurus

LUFENGOSAURUS

> loo-FENG-oh-SAW-rus
? Lufeng reptile
(n) Dr. C. C. Young
(1941)
(m) 38

Triassic period

20ft.

Lufengosaurus is one of the oldest Chinese dinosaurs and it shows that there were prosauropods all over the world. It was closely related to *Plateosaurus*, and was quite large at about 20 feet long. *Lufengosaurus* had a long skull and its teeth were widely spaced. It had long, powerful hind legs and shorter arms—it could probably walk upright on its hind legs or on all fours. The diet of these plateosaurs is a mystery. It has usually been assumed that they ate plants, but the small, spaced teeth had fairly sharp edges and could also have been used for eating meat.

Several skeletons of *Lufengosaurus* were collected by Chinese expeditions to Sichuan and Yunnan provinces in the 1930s and 1940s. Since then, numerous other specimens have been found in various parts of China.

Lufengosaurus

LYCORHINUS

Jurassic period

> LIE-koe-RINE-us
? Wolf snout
ⓝ Dr. S. H. Haughton (1924)
ⓜ

4ft.

Lycorhinus is an important, but poorly-known, dinosaur. It was one of the early ornithopods—a heterodontosaurid—and its close relatives are *Geranosaurus* and *Heterodontosaurus*. *Lycorhinus* was named in 1924 from a part of the left jaw of a very small dinosaur. It shows a large tusk, and teeth as in *Heterodontosaurus*. At first, it was thought to be an early mammal. It was only recognized as a dinosaur in 1962 when *Heterodontosaurus*, its close relative, was described.

Maiasaura

MAIASAURA

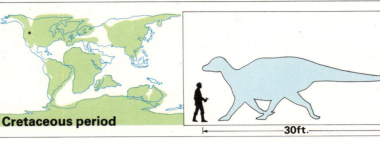

> MY-a-SAW-ra
? Good-mother reptile
ⓝ Dr. J. R. Horner & Mr
R. Makela (1979)
ⓜ 22, 30, 32

Cretaceous period

30ft.

Maiasaura is one of the most important dinosaurs to have been found recently. In 1978 and 1979, skeletons of adult *Maiasaura* were found with nests and babies. The mother was about 30 feet long, and the young animals only 3 feet long. The nests were made in mounds which were 10 feet across, and the eggs were arranged in several layers. In each layer the eggs, which were shaped like sausages, lay in circles like the spokes of a wheel. The mother

Maiasaura clearly laid her eggs carefully, and must have arranged them in this regular pattern. She covered each layer with sand, and then covered the whole nest of eggs so that they were all kept warm until the young ones hatched out. However, the young animals that have been found were not hatchlings, so they were obviously staying around the nest as they grew up. This has suggested that these dinosaurs looked after their young.

Maiasaura's nest: the eggs were laid in a circular pattern in a high mound of earth.

MAJUNGATHOLUS

> ma-YUNG-a-THOL-us

? Dome from Majunga (where found)

(n) Drs. H.-D. Sues & P. Taquet (1979)

(m) 28

Cretaceous period

4½ft.

Majungatholus is known only from a fragment of a domed skull which was found recently on the island of Madagascar, just off the south-eastern coast of Africa. This discovery was completely unexpected since pachycephalosaurs had only been found in the northern hemisphere before then—in North America, Europe, and eastern Asia. Dinosaur fossils are not very common in Madagascar. They include a specimen of *Titanosaurus*, a sauropod, and a very poorly preserved theropod. The *Titanosaurus* specimen is like similar specimens from South America.

Majungatholus was a high-domed pachycephalosaur, like *Stegoceras* and *Pachycephalosaurus* from North America and others from Asia. It seems likely that dinosaurs reached Madagascar from North America via South America and Africa. Someday, pachycephalosaurs may be found in those two continents.

MAMENCHISAURUS

> ma-MENCH-ih-SAW-rus
? Mamenchi (place in China) reptile
(n) Dr. C. C. Young (1954)
(m) 38

Jurassic period

72ft.

Mamenchisaurus was a large sauropod related to *Apatosaurus* and *Diplodocus*. It was known only from some partial skeletons until a nearly complete specimen was found in 1972. This revealed something extraordinary. *Mamenchisaurus* had the longest neck of any animal that has ever lived. The neck was as long as the rest of the body. Out of a total length of 72 feet, 36 feet were neck! There were 19 vertebrae in the neck—the highest number for any

dinosaur—and it was strengthened by rods of bone. It may be that *Mamenchisaurus* stood in the middle of a pond and swept its head around the sides, eating up all the plants, with its neck floating on the water— like a giant vacuum cleaner.

Mamenchisaurus

MASSOSPONDYLUS

> MASS-oh-SPOND-ih-lus
? Massive vertebra
ⓝ Sir Richard Owen
  (1854)
ⓜ 5

Triassic period

13ft.

Massospondylus was a large animal, about 13 feet long, and one of the most widespread early dinosaurs. Its close relatives, which lived at the same time, were *Lufengosaurus* in China and *Plateosaurus* in Europe. *Massospondylus* was named in 1854 by Sir Richard Owen from a few broken vertebrae that had been sent from South Africa to England. New fossils of *Massospondylus* were found later and there are now some partial skeletons from which a reconstruction can be attempted.

Massospondylus was a plant eater. It ate tough leaves, and it had pebbles in its stomach to grind up food, like the grit that birds swallow for the same purpose. It had strong hind legs and arms and its hands could have been used for walking or for grasping. The thumb was huge and it had a large, curved claw. It could be placed against fingers two and three and might have been used for holding things. Fingers four and five were very small. A few odd bones from India have also been named as *Massospondylus*.

Massospondylus

MEGALOSAURUS

> MEG-a-low-SAW-rus
? Great reptile
ⓝ Prof. W. Buckland
  (1824)
ⓜ 52, 59

Jurassic period

30ft.

Megalosaurus was the first dinosaur to be named—in 1824. The first specimens included a jaw bone which contained a number of sharp teeth. These were found in 1818 in slate mines in the village of Stonesfield, near Oxford, England, along with other bones and fossils. It was eventually described after William Buckland *(see pages 14–15)* had tried for some time to find out what it might be.

The teeth of *Megalosaurus* had long roots that fixed them firmly into the jaw bone. The top of the tooth was curved backward and flattened from side to side, and the back and front edges had jagged ridges, like the edge of a steak knife. The hand had three fingers, and the foot four toes, each with a strong claw – *Megalosaurus* was obviously a fearsome predator! About 20 species of *Megalosaurus* have been described, all found in rocks ranging in age over 100 million years. It is unlikely that one species could have survived for so long, and many of the descriptions have been based on very poor finds that could belong to any meat-eating dinosaur.

Megalosaurus

MELANOROSAURUS

> MEL-an-o-roe-SAW-rus
? Black reptile
ⓝ Dr. S. H. Haughton (1924)
ⓜ 1, 5

Triassic period

40ft.

Melanorosaurus was the largest early dinosaur. Its closest relatives were *Euskelosaurus* from South Africa, and *Riojasaurus* from South America, and some people think that these animals are in fact all the same. These melanorosaurids were all huge plant-eaters, but none of the skeletons yet found has had a skull, so they are not well known.

Melanorosaurus probably walked on all fours, unlike its other relatives *Plateosaurus* and *Lufengosaurus* which may have stood upright at times. This suggests that *Melanorosaurus* was more advanced than *Plateosaurus*, and that it had evolved some way toward the later giant sauropods which always walked on all fours. The original specimens of *Melanorosaurus* were a few limb bones and vertebrae —the reconstruction is based on these, and on related forms.

Melanorosaurus

MINMI

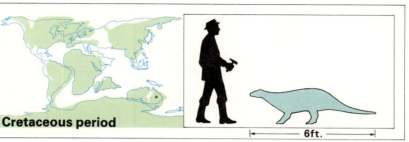

> MIN-mee
? Minmi Crossing
(where found)
ⓝ Dr. R. E. Molnar
(1980)
ⓜ

Cretaceous period

6ft.

The only Australian ankylosaur, *Minmi*, was found in 1964. The remains are very incomplete, and consist of 11 bones from the backbone, a partial foot skeleton, and a large number of armor plates.

The backbone turned out to be very interesting. Each of the bones in the backbone, the vertebrae, had a long, sword-shaped, bony rod that joined it to three or four others behind. This bony rod had a broad, roughly triangular plate of bone in front, and this lay over the top of the rib attachments on a vertebra. Behind this plate ran a long narrow spine of bone, up to 6 inches long. These bone rods seem to have formed within the powerful muscles of the back in *Minmi*, and it has been suggested that they allowed *Minmi* to run fast. The bony rods stiffened the back and took up a great deal of the strain that was produced by the rapidly pounding feet.

Minmi is important since it is the only ankylosaur known from Australia, and indeed it is only one of two known from the southern part of the world. The other comes from India, but has not yet been described.

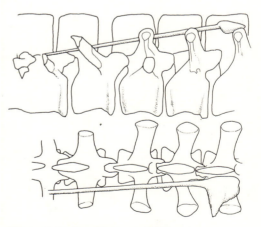

Part of the backbone of *Minmi*, showing one of the special bones that linked the vertebrae together (section shown 7 inches wide).

MONOCLONIUS

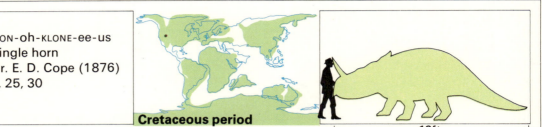

> MON-oh-KLONE-ee-us
? Single horn
ⓝ Dr. E. D. Cope (1876)
ⓜ 7, 25, 30

Cretaceous period

18ft.

Monoclonius was a medium-sized, horned dinosaur about 18 feet long. It is known from several skeletons, and 11 species have been named. *Monoclonius* had a very large horn on its nose, but only slight bumps above its eyes (compare its head with *Triceratops*). The frill was short and its back edge was covered with bony knobs. There were also two bony spikes which pointed forward from the back of the frill.

The first fossils of *Monoclonius* were found as early as 1855 by Ferdinand Hayden during a geological survey of the Judith River area of Montana. These were the first ceratopsian dinosaur remains found anywhere in the world, although this was not clear to Hayden since he had found only fragments of bone and some teeth. Later, some pieces of the bony crest and the single nose horn were collected, and Edward Cope named these remains *Monoclonius* in 1876. Another very similar ceratopsian from Alberta was named *Centrosaurus* in 1904, and it is possible that these two forms are the same kind of animal.

Monoclonius

MUSSAURUS

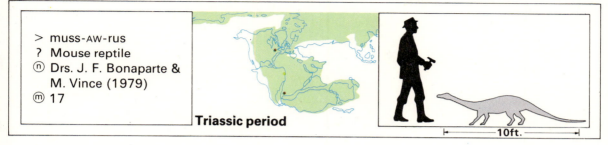

> muss-AW-rus
? Mouse reptile
ⓝ Drs. J. F. Bonaparte & M. Vince (1979)
ⓜ 17

Triassic period

10ft.

Mussaurus was named in 1979, based on five or six small skeletons. These were found together in a nest with the remains of two small eggs. The skeleton shows that *Mussaurus* was a prosauropod, but it is not clear what the adult was like. This is because the bones of a baby dinosaur are different from those of a grownup. The eyes are very big, and the knees and feet seem to be too large, like a puppy.

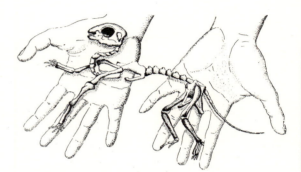

The largest skeleton of Mussaurus was 8 inches long—it could easily fit on to the palms of your hands.

MUTTABURRASAURUS

> MUT-a-BUR-a-SAW-rus
? Muttaburra (where found) reptile
ⓝ Drs. A. Bartholomai & R. E. Molnar (1981)
ⓜ 41

Cretaceous period

23ft.

Muttaburrasaurus is one of the very few dinosaurs known from Australia. It is a recent find and was named in 1981. *Muttaburrasaurus* was 23 feet long and it was related to *Iguanodon* and to *Camptosaurus*. It is an important find since it is one of the few known iguanodontid dinosaurs from the southern part of the world.

Its closest relatives at that time lived in Europe, Asia, and North America.

It had a low, broad head, and it has been suggested that its teeth could have been used for chopping plants or meat. Like most Late Cretaceous ornithopods, *Muttaburrasaurus* was larger than its Early Jurassic counterparts.

NEMEGTOSAURUS

> nem-EGT-oh-SAW-rus
? Nemegt (where found) reptile
Ⓝ Dr. A. Nowiński (1971)
Ⓜ 39, 50

Cretaceous period

size unknown

Nemegtosaurus is known only from a skull which looks like that of *Diplodocus*. This specimen was collected in 1965 by a joint Polish-Mongolian expedition to the Gobi Desert, Mongolia. The skull is long and it slopes forward. Like other diplodocids, *Nemegtosaurus* had only a small number of peg-like teeth at the front of its jaws. If *Nemegtosaurus* is a diplodocid, it lived much later than its relatives which all come from rocks dated as 50 million years older. The headless skeleton of another sauropod, *Opisthocoelicaudia*, was found in the same deposit as the head of *Nemegtosaurus*, and it has been suggested that the two might go together as one animal. However, the skeleton of *Opisthocoelicaudia* is more like that of a camarasaurid than a diplodocid.

NOASAURUS

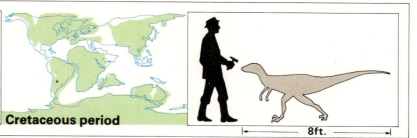

- > NOE-a-SAW-rus
- ? North-west Argentina reptile
- ⓝ Drs. J. F. Bonaparte & J. Powell (1980)
- ⓜ 17

Cretaceous period

8ft.

The slashing claw of *Noasaurus*, showing the special pit at the back for the attachment of a powerful muscle (claw 1½ inches long).

Nemegtosaurus

Noasaurus was a medium-sized, active hunting dinosaur. It was named in 1980 on the basis of some parts of a skull, some vertebrae, and two foot bones. It had a fierce, hooked claw on its foot, just like *Deinonychus* and *Dromaeosaurus*, and it used this to attack other dinosaurs. The claw had a broad outer curve, and a strange "lumpy" curve on the inside. This lay around a special pit near the top of the claw which would have had a strong muscle attached in life. This muscle gave the claw great strength.

The skull of *Noasaurus* is rather different from that of *Deinonychus*, although the claw might have suggested that *Noasaurus* was a deinonychosaur. The Argentinian scientists who named *Noasaurus* could find no other known dinosaur which they could regard as a close relative, and they argued that it represented an entirely new group, the noasaurids. It is interesting to see that the deinonychosaurs and the noasaurids evolved the same type of slashing claw separately.

NODOSAURUS

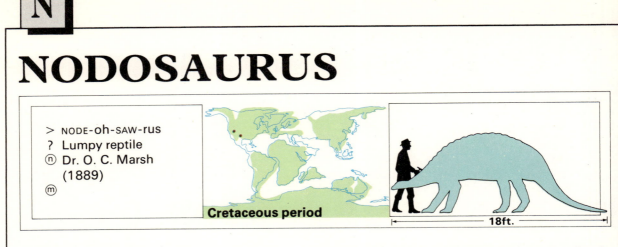

> NODE-oh-SAW-rus
? Lumpy reptile
ⓝ Dr. O. C. Marsh (1889)
ⓜ

Cretaceous period

18ft.

Nodosaurus was a medium-sized, armored dinosaur related to *Panoplosaurus* and *Silvisaurus*. It had an armor of small bony knobs which were set in its skin all over the body. On the back and hip region were some oval-shaped plates which had small spines. These bony plates and spines were not attached to the bones of the skeleton—they sat in the animal's tough skin. This makes it difficult to know exactly how they were arranged. This armor must have been very heavy, and *Nodosaurus* had powerful limbs to support the weight.

Nodosaurus was first mentioned by Othniel C. Marsh in 1889 on the basis of a few fragments of a skeleton. However, it was only described fully in 1921 by R. S. Lull after new specimens had been found in Wyoming and Kansas. Unfortunately, the head is completely unknown. *Nodosaurus* was 16 to 19 feet long.

Nodosaurus

OPISTHOCOELICAUDIA

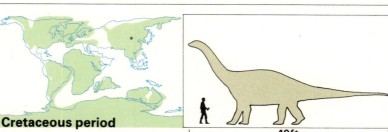

> oh-PIS-thoe-SEEL-ih-KOW-dee-a
? Tail bones hollow at the back
ⁿ Dr. M. Borsuk-Bialynicka (1977)
ᵐ 39, 50

Cretaceous period

40ft.

Opisthocoelicaudia was a moderate-sized sauropod, about 40 feet long. Only the skeleton is known, but this shows that it was related to *Camarasaurus* and *Euhelopus*. The skeleton was found in 1965 during a joint Polish-Mongolian expedition to the Gobi Desert, Mongolia. The head and neck of *Opisthocoelicaudia* were not found, and it has been suggested that the *Nemegtosaurus* head might belong with it.

It seems likely that the head and neck of *Opisthocoelicaudia* were lost because the body had been damaged before it turned into a fossil. The dead dinosaur may have been damaged by river waters, or by flesh-eating dinosaurs, which removed the head and neck. Some of the leg bones show tooth marks where they may have been bitten through by a tyrannosaurid meat-eating dinosaur. This left only the body, tail, and legs to be preserved. The tail bones of *Opisthocoelicaudia* show that it might have been able to use its tail to grasp things, or to act as a prop.

Opisthocoelicaudia

ORNITHISCHIA

The order Ornithischia includes a broad range of dinosaurs, all of which were plant eaters. There were two-legged animals like *Iguanodon* and the duckbills (ornithopods), the thick-headed dinosaurs (pachycephalosaurs), and the three groups of armored dinosaurs (stegosaurs, ankylosaurs, and ceratopsians). The Ornithischia evolved later than the other dinosaur order, the Saurischia, which was first represented in the Late Triassic.

The oldest ornithischian suborder, the Ornithopoda, survived from the Early Jurassic right to the end of the Cretaceous, and included dinosaurs such as *Fabrosaurus*, *Heterodontosaurus*, and *Scutellosaurus*. Dinosaurs from this suborder seem to have been the predecessors of the horned ceratopsians and the dome-headed pachycephalosaurs, but it is not certain when these species evolved. These two groups are known only from the later part of the Cretaceous.

The other ornithischian groups, the plated stegosaurs and the armored ankylosaurs arose in the Middle Jurassic, but were quite rare until the Cretaceous. The stegosaurs and the ankylosaurs seem to have shared a common ancestor, possibly something rather like *Scelidosaurus* from the Early Jurassic.

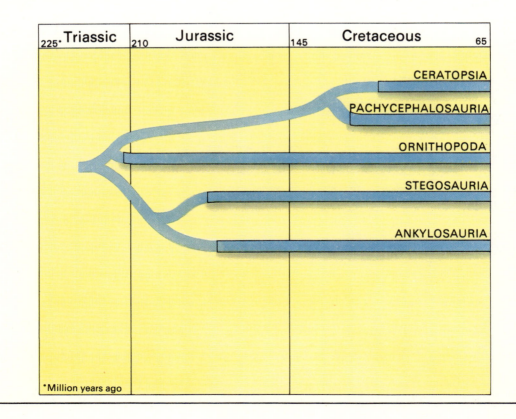

225* Triassic	210 Jurassic	145 Cretaceous 65

CERATOPSIA

PACHYCEPHALOSAURIA

ORNITHOPODA

STEGOSAURIA

ANKYLOSAURIA

*Million years ago

ORNITHOLESTES

> or-NITH-oh-LESS-teez
? Bird robber
ⓝ Prof. H. F. Osborn
(1903)
ⓜ 7, 32

Triassic period

6ft.

Ornitholestes was a small, lightly-built meat eater. An almost complete skeleton, found in 1900 in the famous dinosaur beds of Wyoming, shows that it was 6 feet long. Since 1900, only one other specimen of *Ornitholestes*, an incomplete hand, has been found. The legs and arms were slim and long. *Ornitholestes* had small teeth and rather weak hands. It was clearly a fast runner, and may have fed on small animals like lizards, frogs, and early mammals, which lived at that time. *Ornitholestes* is very similar to *Coelurus*.

Ornitholestes

ORNITHOMIMOSAURIA

The infraorder Ornithomimosauria is made up of a group of advanced, active, running dinosaurs.

It is possible that the first representatives of this infraorder evolved in the Late Jurassic. *Elaphrosaurus* from Tanzania in East Africa, had the long slender limbs and ostrich-like body of later ornithomimosaurs, but its head is not known. This means that it is impossible to check for the key ornithomimosaur characteristics found in the head—large brain, large eyes, and no teeth. Another very doubtful ornithomimosaur is *Deinocheirus*, known only from a pair of huge arms with great claws. Definite ornithomimosaurs all date from the Late Cretaceous of North America *(Ornithomimus, Struthiomimus)* and central Asia *(Avimimus, Oviraptor)*.

Most dinosaurs in this infraorder are members of the family Ornithomimosauridae. However, *Oviraptor* is so distinctive, with its strange short head and nose bump, that it is placed in a separate family, the Oviraptoridae. *Avimimus* is even more of a problem. It has the lightly-built, birdlike body of the ornithomimosaurs, but the hand and skull are too poorly known to say whether they were like those of *Ornithomimus*. Until more fossils are found, *Avimimus* is placed in its own family, the Avimimidae.

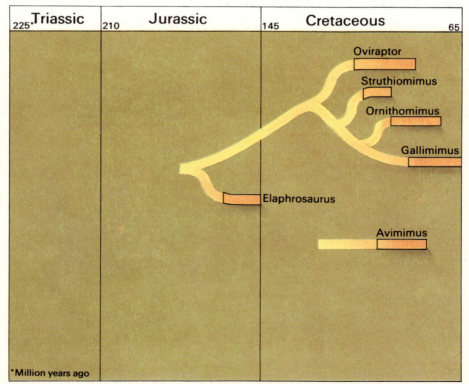

225 Triassic	210 Jurassic	145 Cretaceous 65

Oviraptor
Struthiomimus
Ornithomimus
Gallimimus
Elaphrosaurus
Avimimus

*Million years ago

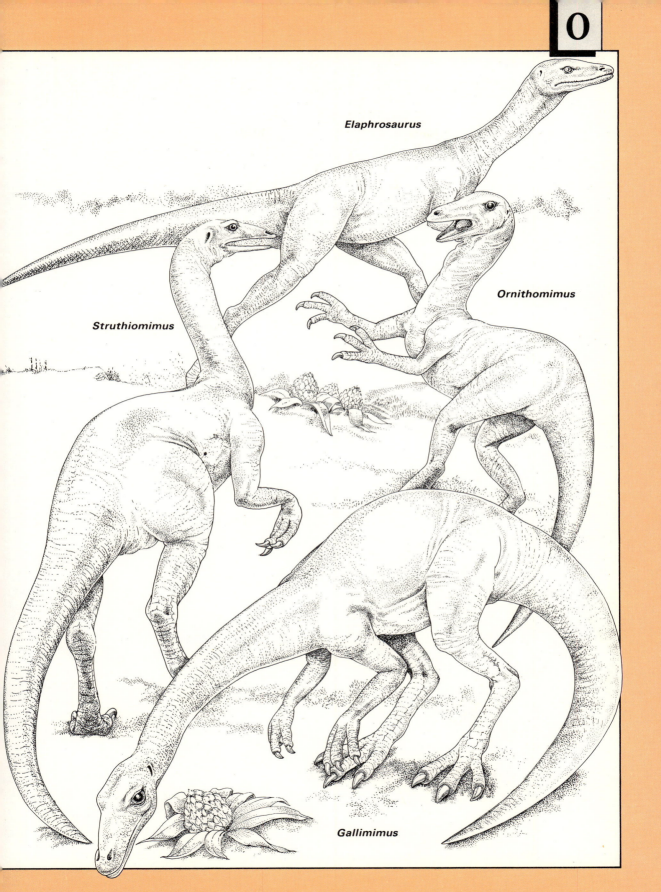

Elaphrosaurus

Ornithomimus

Struthiomimus

Gallimimus

ORNITHOMIMUS

> or-NITH-oh-MIME-us
? Bird mimic
(n) Dr. O. C. Marsh (1890)
(m) 29

Cretaceous period

11ft.

Ornithomimus

Ornithomimus was a medium-sized, ostrich dinosaur. More than half of its length of 10 to 13 feet was tail. Many skeletons and odd bones of *Ornithomimus* have been found, and ten species have been described. The first remains were found in 1889 near Denver, Colorado, and they were named by Othniel C. Marsh. He described several species, all on the basis of poor remains. It was only in 1917 that a reasonably complete skeleton of *Struthiomimus*, its close relative, was described. This showed what the missing parts of *Ornithomimus* were probably like. *Ornithomimus* had no teeth, but probably had a horny beak. It may have gathered food such as leaves, fruit, roots, insects, lizards, and small mammals using its long strong fingers. It could chop these and swallow them in chunks, just as birds do. *Ornithomimus* is closely related to *Struthiomimus*, but differs in the relative length of the limbs and the shape of the hands.

ORNITHOPODA

225*Triassic	210 Jurassic	145 Cretaceous 65
		Anatosaurus
		Edmontosaurus
		Brachylophosaurus
		Hadrosaurus
		Claosaurus
		Secernosaurus
		Shantungosaurus
		Saurolophus
		Prosaurolophus
		Maiasaura
		Tsintaosaurus
		Parasaurolophus
		Corythosaurus
		Lambeosaurus
		Hypacrosaurus

*Million years ago

103

ORNITHOPODA

The suborder Ornithopoda includes 60 to 70 different plant-eating dinosaurs. The Ornithopoda evolved at the beginning of the Jurassic. The two earliest families were the Fabrosauridae and Heterodontosauridae, all small animals known mainly from southern Africa *(Fabrosaurus, Geranosaurus)* and North America *(Scutellosaurus)*, with a recent find from China *(Xiaosaurus)*. The third ornithopod family, the Hypsilophodontidae, is known mainly from the Late Jurassic and Early Cretaceous of North America *(Dryosaurus, Zephyrosaurus)* Europe *(Hypsilophodon)* and Africa *(Dryosaurus)*. The family Iguanodontidae arose in the Late Jurassic of America *(Camptosaurus)* and spread to Europe, Africa, and Australia.

In the Late Cretaceous the largest ornithopod family, the Hadrosauridae (duck-billed dinosaurs), rose to dominate as plant eaters in most parts of the world. Some of the hadrosaurs had no crests; these are known especially from North America *(Anatosaurus, Hadrosaurus)*, Asia *(Shantungosaurus)*, and South America *(Secernosaurus)*. The best-known hadrosaurs, however, had various types of crests; these include a large number of forms from North America *(Corythosaurus, Lambeosaurus, Maiasaura)* and Asia *(Saurolophus, Tsintaosaurus)*.

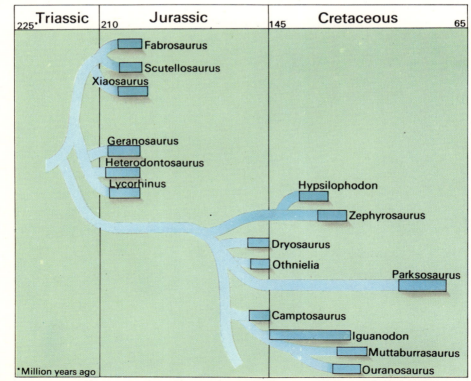

| 225*Triassic | 210 | Jurassic | 145 | Cretaceous | 65 |

Fabrosaurus
Scutellosaurus
Xiaosaurus
Geranosaurus
Heterodontosaurus
Lycorhinus
Hypsilophodon
Zephyrosaurus
Dryosaurus
Othnielia
Parksosaurus
Camptosaurus
Iguanodon
Muttaburrasaurus
Ouranosaurus

*Million years ago

Parasaurolophus

Anatosaurus

ryosaurus

Hypsilophodon

Heterodontosaurus

OURANOSAURUS

> oo-RAN-oh-SAW-rus
? Brave reptile
ⓝ Dr. P. Taquet (1976)
ⓜ 2, 51, 55, 58

Cretaceous period

23ft.

Ouranosaurus is one of the most interesting dinosaurs from North Africa. It was related to *Iguanodon*, but had a tall sail down its back. The sail was supported by the spines of the backbone—one on each vertebra. The sail was made of skin, and blood vessels must have flowed through it. It may have been used by *Ouranosaurus* to keep its body temperature constant. If it was too hot, it could lose heat through the sail, and if it was too cold, it could take in heat from the sun. There is clear evidence that *Ouranosaurus* lived in warm and dry conditions from the sediments in which the bones were found. Another dinosaur with a sail was the meat-eater *Spinosaurus*.

In most other respects, *Ouranosaurus* was very like *Iguanodon*, and it would be hard to tell individual bones from both forms apart. *Ouranosaurus* had smaller hands, and its head was a slightly different shape, with a lower snout and a thinner jaw.

Ouranosaurus

OVIRAPTOR

> OVE-ih-RAP-tor
? Egg thief
ⓝ Prof. H. F. Osborn
(1924)
ⓜ 39

Cretaceous period

5–6ft.

Oviraptor was an unusually small coelurosaur. The first skeleton was found in 1923 just above a nest of *Protoceratops* eggs, and it was thought that *Oviraptor* was an egg eater for this reason. It had a short head and a powerful, toothless beak that might have been covered with a horny sheath, just like a bird's beak. There was also a bony bump or crest over the snout. The jaws were curved so that it could crush very hard objects. *Oviraptor* had strong three-fingered hands with large claws which may have been useful for grasping things. *Oviraptor* may have eaten eggs, but the powerful beak suggests that it could have crushed bones. The closest relatives of *Oviraptor* seem to have been *Ornithomimus* and *Struthiomimus*, but they had more slender skulls.

Oviraptor

PACHYCEPHALOSAURIA

The suborder Pachycephalosauria was only recently named as a group of two-legged, plant-eating dinosaurs with enormously thick skull roofs. The skull roof was up to 10 inches thick, and for that reason, this part of the animal was easily fossilized. Many of the boneheads are only known from these skull roofs, and detailed studies have shown that they may have been used in head-butting. Although the pachycephalosaurs did not have horns, it is now thought that they charged at each other, just as some sheep and cattle do today. The force of the blow was taken up by the thick bony cranium which protected the brain, but would have run down the backbone which was also specially strengthened. Male sheep and wild cattle often butt heads with rivals in order to decide which is the strongest, and as a result, head of the herd. This may tell us something about how the pachycephalosaurs behaved. Did they live in herds of 20 or so animals, with a dominant male in charge?

Pachycephalosaurs may have arisen in the Early Cretaceous in Europe (there is a single poor specimen from the south of England), but they are best known from the Late Cretaceous of North America (*Pachycephalosaurus, Stegoceras*) and Asia (*Goyocephale, Homalocephale*), with a remarkable new find from the island of Madagascar, just off the east coast of Africa—a dinosaur named *Majungatholus*.

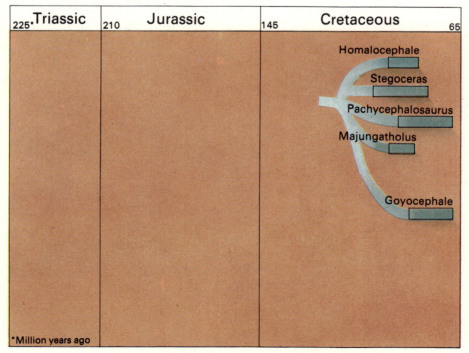

225.Triassic	210 Jurassic	145 Cretaceous 65

Homalocephale
Stegoceras
Pachycephalosaurus
Majungatholus
Goyocephale

*Million years ago

Pachycephalosaurus

Homalocephale

Stegoceras

P

PACHYCEPHALOSAURUS

> PAK-ee-KEF-al-oh-SAW-rus

? Thick-headed reptile

Ⓝ Drs. B. Brown & E. M. Schlaikjer (1943)

Ⓜ

Cretaceous period

26ft.

Pachycephalosaurus was a large bonehead. It was probably far bigger than its relatives – up to 26 feet long—although its whole skeleton has not been found. The skull has a very thick top, just behind and above the eyes, and is ornamented with knobs and spines at the front and the back of the neck. It seems that *Pachycephalosaurus* used its crash helmet head when fighting with other members of its own species. Today, male deer and goats batter each other head-on, fighting for mates, and paleontologists believe that this is just what *Pachycephalosaurus* did.

Pachycephalosaurus

PACHYRHINOSAURUS

> PAK-ee-RINE-oh-SAW-rus
? Thick-nosed reptile
ⓝ Dr. C. M. Sternberg (1950)
ⓜ 32

Cretaceous period

18ft.

Pachyrhinosaurus is one of the most unusual horned dinosaurs. It is known from only two skulls and a few other pieces. *Pachyrhinosaurus* was a large animal: its skull alone measured up to 5 feet long, and its body may have been up to 18 feet long.

Pachyrhinosaurus had a short neck frill at the back of the skull, but no horns, only a thick mass of bone in the middle of its snout between the eyes. It has been suggested that this rough patch of bone could actually have been produced after a normal ceratopsian horn had been broken off. If this is the case, then *Pachyrhinosaurus* would not be a separate form of dinosaur.

PANOPLOSAURUS

> pan-o-ploe-SAW-rus
? Fully armoured reptile
ⓝ Dr L. M. Lambe (1919)
ⓜ 7, 24

Cretaceous period

23ft.

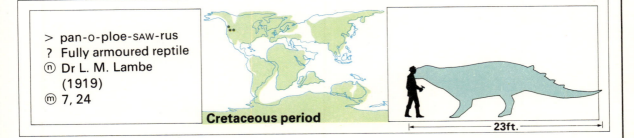

Panoplosaurus was one of the last surviving ankylosaurs. It is known from a partial skull and skeleton. Its head was massive, and the top of the skull was arched and covered with large armor plates. These plates covered over the normal bones of the skull as a second outer layer, and they also ran down the side of the skull, making the eye socket quite small. *Panoplosaurus* had a narrow snout and small, ridged teeth, and it may have fed by selecting plants at ground level.

PARASAUROLOPHUS

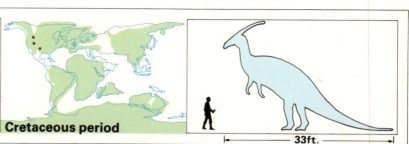

> par-a-SAWR-oh-LOAF-
us
? Reptile with parallel-
sided crest
ⓝ Dr. W. Parks (1923)
ⓜ 16, 29

Cretaceous period

33ft.

Parasaurolophus was one of the most bizarre, duck-billed dinosaurs. It had a long tubular crest that curved back from its snout for a distance of up to 6 feet. This crest seems to have been much longer in the males than the females. The nostrils were in their normal place at the front of the snout, and the breathing tubes ran right up the crest and back down again into the mouth. If you cut the crest open, you would find four tubes—two going up and two coming down. The crest may have been a signal to let other *Parasaurolophus* recognize a member of their own species. If *Parasaurolophus* breathed out strongly, it could have made a honk or bellow inside the crest.

Parasaurolophus had strong arms which were probably used for walking and for swimming. The tail was long and flattened from side to side. It could have been used for swimming by beating sideways.

Parasaurolophus

PARKSOSAURUS

> PARKS-oh-SAW-rus
? Parks' (Canadian palaeontologist) reptile
(n) Dr. C. M. Sternberg (1937)
(m)

Cretaceous period

8ft.

Parksosaurus was one of the last surviving hypsilophodontids. Its ancestors include *Dryosaurus*, *Hypsilophodon*, and *Zephyrosaurus* which all lived 50 million years earlier in the Late Jurassic and Early Cretaceous periods. *Parksosaurus* is known only from an incomplete skull because when this animal died it was buried on its left side in the sand, and most of the right-hand side of the skull was broken up and lost. It was first described in 1913 as belonging to another form, and it was only in 1937 that Charles Sternberg realized that this was a new species of dinosaur. *Parksosaurus* had large eyes with special bones to support the eyelids and the huge eyeball itself. These small bones are often found in ornithopods.

PATAGOSAURUS

> pat-AJ-oh-SAW-rus
? Patagonian reptile
(n) Dr. J. F. Bonaparte (1979)
(m) 17

Jurassic period

60ft.

Patagosaurus was named in 1979 on the basis of five incomplete skeletons that had been found during expeditions led by Dr. José Bonaparte to northern Argentina in 1977, 1982, and 1983. The most complete skeleton is a large adult animal, consisting of 24 bones from the backbone, various ribs, and some bones of the limbs. Other skeletons come from fully grown, partially grown, and quite young animals. The only parts of the head that were found were two jaws from the youngest animal. These show long, peg-like teeth which are typical of most sauropods. The bones of the backbone show that *Patagosaurus* was a very large animal.

PELOROSAURUS

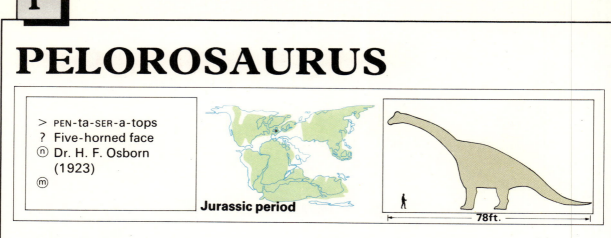

> PEN-ta-SER-a-tops
? Five-horned face
ⓝ Dr. H. F. Osborn
   (1923)

ⓜ

Jurassic period

78ft.

Pelorosaurus was a large animal, related to *Brachiosaurus* and *"Supersaurus."* It may have had an armor of little bone plates ($\frac{1}{2}$ to 1 inch across) sunk into its skin. This name was given by Gideon Mantell (who also named *Iguanodon* and *Hylaeosaurus*) in 1850 to a partial arm bone found in Sussex, southern England. Since then, dozens of fragments of sauropods of about the same age have been given the name *Pelorosaurus*—about 20 species in all.

It is a common problem that the poorer the specimens are, the more names they are given. The remains of *Pelorosaurus* include odd teeth, bones of the arm and leg, isolated bones from the backbone, ribs, and various fragments from dozens of different places in the south of England. The names that were given to these specimens between 1850 and 1900 include *Chondrosteosaurus, Dinodocus, Eucamerotus, Gigantosaurus, Hoplosaurus, Ischyrosaurus, Morinosaurus, Neosodon, Oplosaurus,* and *Ornithopsis*. Later studies have shown that it is much more likely that these are all scattered pieces of just one species of giant sauropod that lived in the south of England at the time of *Iguanodon* and *Baryonyx*.

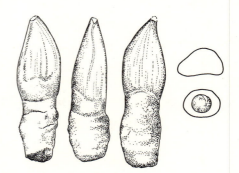

Three views of a tooth of Pelorosaurus, and two cross-sections. The tooth was found on the Isle of Wight, southern England (tooth $3\frac{3}{8}$ inches long).

PENTACERATOPS

Cretaceous period

23ft.

Pentaceratops had more horns than the other horned dinosaurs—five in all. It had one on its snout, one above each eye, and one on each cheek, at the bottom of the frill. In fact, only three of these are really horns: the cheek "spikes" are found in all ceratopsians but are simply slightly larger than normal in *Pentaceratops*. This array of horns was used for defense against meat-eating dinosaurs. It is also likely that *Pentaceratops* used its horns for display. The neck frill was very long, and the back edge was knobby because of pointed pieces of bone set into the edge. *Pentaceratops* was related to *Anchiceratops* and *Torosaurus*, and it may have been as much as 23 feet long.

Pentaceratops

PIATNITZKYSAURUS

> pee-at-NITS-kee-SAW-rus
? Piatnitzky's (fossil collector) reptile
(n) Dr. J. F. Bonaparte (1979)
(m) 17

Jurassic period

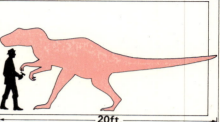

20ft.

Piatnitzkysaurus is known from a fairly complete skeleton and a few other pieces which were collected during the same expeditions to northern Argentina in 1977, 1982, and 1983 that produced the remains of *Patagosaurus*. The skull is not very well known, but it can be seen that *Piatnitzkysaurus* had long, pointed, meat-eating teeth, just like *Allosaurus* and *Ceratosaurus*, both North American dinosaurs of that period. *Piatnitzkysaurus* had powerful hind legs and shorter arms, so it is likely that it ran upright on its hind legs. There were four toes on the foot, and probably three fingers on the hand, like *Allosaurus*, but the hand is completely unknown in *Piatnitzkysaurus*. Most features of the skull and skeleton show that this new Argentinian carnosaur is very similar to *Allosaurus*.

Piatnitzkysaurus

PINACOSAURUS

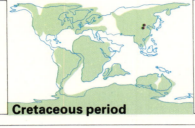

> pin-AK-oh-SAW-rus
? Plank reptile
Ⓝ Dr. C. W. Gilmore
  (1933)
Ⓜ 50

Cretaceous period

16ft.

Pinacosaurus was a large, lightly-built armored dinosaur. It had a rounded beak and the top of its skull was covered with small, bony plates. A skull of a young *Pinacosaurus* shows that these plates were separate at first, gradually fusing together into a solid heavy sheet of bone in the adult. Its eye was set quite far back, and its teeth were very small. *Pinacosaurus* was remarkable for a pair of small openings in the skull near the nostrils, but the purpose of these is not known. The front of the skull was curved down to form a pointed, parrot-like beak.

   Pinacosaurus was related to *Ankylosaurus* and *Dyoplosaurus*, and it was 16 feet long. Its remains were collected on expeditions to Mongolia in the 1920s mounted by the American Museum of Natural History (New York).

Pinacosaurus skull (21 inches wide).

PLATEOSAURUS

> PLAT-ee-oh-SAW-rus
? Flat reptile
ⓝ Dr. H. von Meyer
   (1837)
ⓜ 7, 19, 49, 63, 64

Triassic period

26ft.

Plateosaurus is the most common early prosauropod dinosaur known. Dozens of skeletons of this large 26-foot-long animal have been collected all over central Europe (in West Germany, East Germany, France, and Switzerland) from 50 or more different places. Some of these are beautifully preserved.

Plateosaurus had a fairly long, light skull with small, leaf-shaped teeth spaced out along its jaws. It had quite a long neck and strong limbs. *Plateosaurus* had broad hands with a large, curved thumb claw which it probably used to rake up leaves to eat. It could have moved on all fours, or reared up on its hind legs to feed in trees. Some scientists have even suggested recently that *Plateosaurus* might have eaten meat, but this is unlikely.

Plateosaurus

PROCOMPSOGNATHUS

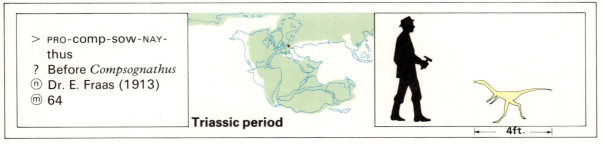

> PRO-comp-sow-NAY-thus
? Before *Compsognathus*
ⓝ Dr. E. Fraas (1913)
ⓜ 64

Triassic period

4ft.

Procompsognathus was a very small, early dinosaur. It was an agile, running meat eater that probably fed on small lizardlike animals and insects. The skull of *Procompsognathus* was only 3 inches long; it had large eyes and pointed curved teeth. Unfortunately, only one incomplete specimen is known of this important early form. *Procompsognathus* is related to *Coelophysis*, *Saltopus*, and *Syntarsus*.

Procompsognathus

PROSAUROLOPHUS

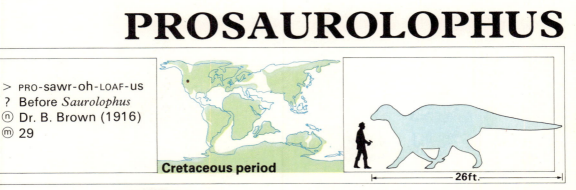

> PRO-sawr-oh-LOAF-us
? Before *Saurolophus*
ⓝ Dr. B. Brown (1916)
ⓜ 29

Cretaceous period

26ft.

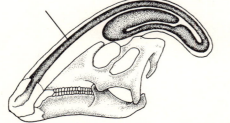

Prosaurolophus skull (including spine, 3 feet long).

Prosaurolophus was a large, duck-billed dinosaur, up to 26 feet long. The skull was low and had a small crest which ran up from the tip of the snout. There was a small knob at the top of this, just in front of the eyes. Compared to many of the duckbills this was a tiny crest.

PROSAUROPODA

The infraorder Prosauropoda is made up of a selection of medium- and large-sized dinosaurs that date from the Late Triassic and the Early Jurassic. They all show that they evolved from two-legged ancestors.

The Prosauropoda was the second major dinosaur group to appear after the Coelurosauria. Some of the earliest so-called "prosauropods," like *Ischisaurus* and *Staurikosaurus*, both from South America, were probably not prosauropods at all, but primitive dinosaurs that were the predecessors of all later forms. Three families of true prosauropods arose in the Late Triassic. First, the relatively small anchisaurids, like *Anchisaurus* from North America and South Africa, and *Thecodontosaurus* from Europe, became quite important. Then the larger plateosaurids rose to greater importance, with forms like *Plateosaurus* in Europe, *Lufengosaurus* in Asia, *Massospondylus* in South Africa, and possibly also *Ammosaurus* in North America, and *Mussaurus* in South America. The largest prosauropods, the melanorosaurids, lived mainly in the Early Jurassic of southern Africa *(Euskelosaurus, Melanorosaurus, Vulcanodon)*, with probable relatives in South America and China. These intriguing animals are still poorly known since most of them consist only of collections of large limb bones, and little is known of the skull.

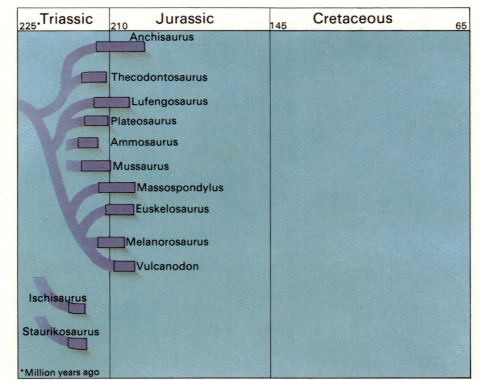

225•Triassic 210 Jurassic 145 Cretaceous 65

Anchisaurus
Thecodontosaurus
Lufengosaurus
Plateosaurus
Ammosaurus
Mussaurus
Massospondylus
Euskelosaurus
Melanorosaurus
Vulcanodon
Ischisaurus
Staurikosaurus

•Million years ago

Lufengosaurus

Plateosaurus

Melanorosaurus

Anchisaurus

PROTOCERATOPS

> pro-toe-SER-a-tops
? First horned-face
ⓝ Drs. W. Granger & W. K. Gregory (1923)
ⓜ 7, 9, 13, 39, 50, 51, 57, 60, 63

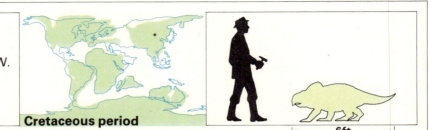

Cretaceous period

6ft.

Protoceratops is the best-known, early, horned dinosaur. Many skeletons were collected during an American expedition to Mongolia in 1922. Some of these were found with complete nests of eggs—one of the first examples of how dinosaurs produced their young. There were skeletons of baby *Protoceratops*, some still unhatched within the eggs. Adult *Protoceratops* was 6 feet long: the babies were 1 foot long.

Protoceratops had a pointed beak and a small neck frill. It had no horns, unlike later ceratopsians, but there were thickened areas of bone on top of the snout and above the eyes. Its closest relatives were *Bagaceratops*, *Leptoceratops*, and *Microceratops*. *Protoceratops* is often said to be an early form of the later horned dinosaurs. Although it walked on all fours it had very long hind legs, which shows that it once went on two legs, as *Psittacosaurus* did.

Protoceratops

PSITTACOSAURUS

> si-TAK-oh-SAW-rus
? Parrot reptile
ⓝ Dr. H. F. Osborn (1923)
ⓜ 7, 8, 38, 39, 60

Cretaceous period

6ft.

Psittacosaurus is an interesting animal: it seems to be partly an ornithopod and partly a horned dinosaur. *Psittacosaurus* had long hind legs and shorter arms, so that it probably walked upright like *Iguanodon*. However, the skull was a little like that of an early ceratopsian (*Leptoceratops* for example). *Psittacosaurus* had a horny beak, a massive short snout, a deep jaw, and a small frill at the back with short spines pointing backward. One species had a small horn on its nose.

The first specimens, two incomplete skeletons, were collected on the American expeditions to Mongolia between 1922 and 1925. These were named *Psittacosaurus* and *Protiguanodon* originally, but it has since been shown that both skeletons belonged to the same form.

Psittacosaurus

RHOETOSAURUS

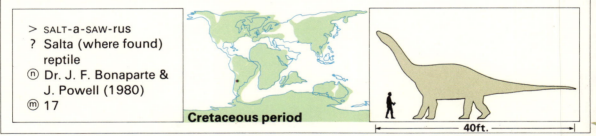

> REET-oh-SAW-rus
? Rhoetos (A Greek mythical giant) reptile
ⓝ Dr. H. A. Longman (1926)
ⓜ 41

Jurassic period

40ft.

Rhoetosaurus is a poorly-known, early sauropod from Australia. The skeleton was dug up in two parts: a tail in 1924, and the hip region in 1926. These bones were not enough to reconstruct *Rhoetosaurus* completely, but its length has been estimated at 40 feet. This might be an underestimate, because the discovery of a single long neck bone suggests that *Rhoetosaurus* probably had a long neck. Its thigh bone was 5 feet long.

Rhoetosaurus is one of the oldest sauropods, and it is probably related to *Cetiosaurus*, *Barapasaurus*, *Vulcanodon*, and *Patagosaurus*. It seems that these early sauropods had managed to spread to all parts of the world in the Early and Middle Jurassic.

SALTASAURUS

> SALT-a-SAW-rus
? Salta (where found) reptile
ⓝ Dr. J. F. Bonaparte & J. Powell (1980)
ⓜ 17

Cretaceous period

40ft.

Saltasaurus was a large, armored sauropod. Five incomplete skeletons of this animal were found in the late 1970s and these show that it was related to *Antarctosaurus* and *Titanosaurus*. Much of the skeleton of *Saltasaurus* is still unknown, but it can be seen that it had unusual vertebrae in the backbone. The most interesting thing about *Saltasaurus* is that thousands of small and large bone plates were found with the skeletons. The small plates were only $\frac{1}{5}$ inch or so across and they were packed closely in the skin to cover the whole body. The large plates were up to 4 inches across, and they had a ridge in the middle. This was the first discovery of armor plates belonging to a sauropod.

SALTOPUS

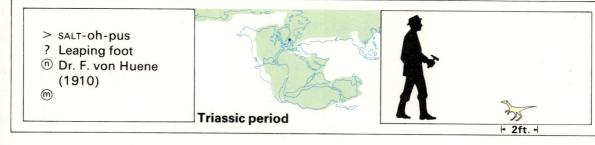

> SALT-oh-pus
? Leaping foot
ⓝ Dr. F. von Huene (1910)
ⓜ

Triassic period

2ft.

Saltopus is one of the oldest dinosaurs known. It was named in 1910 from a small skeleton found in a sandstone quarry. *Saltopus* was an agile little animal, only 2 feet long, and it may have fed on small, lizardlike animals and insects. *Saltopus* had long hind legs, and it was thought to be a jumping animal. However, it probably simply ran, like its relatives *Coelophysis* and *Procompsognathus*.

Unfortunately, its remains are incomplete, lacking the skull and parts of the limbs, and they are very poorly preserved. Much of the fossil bone material has been lost and there are only hollows left in the rock. It has to be studied from artificial casts made from the rock molds. *Saltopus* could be the oldest dinosaur from Europe, and one of the oldest in the world, but it will be hard to say what it looked like until more specimens are found.

Saltopus

SAURISCHIA

The order Saurischia includes all the meat-eating dinosaurs, and the large, heavy, long-necked plant eaters. It is divided into two suborders, the Theropoda (small and large meat eaters), and the Sauropodomorpha (medium and large plant eaters). The main groups of saurischian dinosaurs are listed under "Sauropodomorpha" and "Theropoda" in this guide.

The origins of the Saurischia have recently been discussed a great deal. Until a few years ago, most dinosaur experts believed that the dinosaurs arose from three or more ancestors— one for the Ornithischia, one for the Sauropodomorpha, and one for the Theropoda. When you compare typical dinosaurs from each of these groups, it is easy to see how this idea arose, because they all look very different from each other. However, more detailed studies of the very earliest dinosaurs—*Anchisaurus, Coelophysis, Plateosaurus, Staurikosaurus*—have shown that they are not so different. They all share a large number of specialized characteristics in the hip region, the hind leg, the ankle, and the foot, as well as other parts of the body. It now seems clear that all dinosaurs arose from a single ancestor near the end of the Middle Triassic, and that the Saurischia also evolved from a single ancestor a little later on, after the Ornithischia had branched off.

225·Triassic	210	Jurassic	145	Cretaceous	65
				SAUROPODOMORPHA	
				THEROPODA	

*Million years ago

SAUROLOPHUS

> SAWR-oh-LOAF-us
? Ridged reptile
ⓝ Dr. B. Brown (1912)
ⓜ 7, 60

Cretaceous period

30–33ft.

Saurolophus was an advanced, crested, duck-billed dinosaur. It is known from several skeletons which show an animal about 30 to 33 feet long. *Saurolophus* had a large head with a pointed crest running backward. The snout was broad, and the top of the head sloped backward as a flat surface. Above the eyes, the skull bones continued backward as a spike which stuck out behind the head. It is likely that *Saurolophus* had loose skin over the top of its snout which could be blown up like a balloon. When the air came out, *Saurolophus* would have made a great bellow.

The North American and Asian species of *Saurolophus* were very similar except that the Asian one had a longer skull and a longer crest. As in other duckbills, the front of the jaws had no teeth. Plant food was grasped between the bony duckbills at the front, and pulled back by the large tongue to be chewed.

Saurolophus

SAUROPODA

Apatosaurus

Cetiosaurus

Diplodoc

Brachiosaurus

Camarasaurus

The infraorder Sauropoda includes all of the big, long-necked, plant-eating dinosaurs. There were probably five main groups which can be told apart by features of the backbone (vertebrae), legs, and head: the cetiosaurids, the brachiosaurids, the camarasaurids, the titanosaurids, and the diplodocids.

The first sauropods, the cetiosaurids of the Early Jurassic of India *(Barapasaurus)* and Australia *(Rhoetosaurus)*, are not well known, but they seem to be similar to some of the advanced prosauropods, such as *Melanorosaurus* and *Vulcanodon*. The brachiosaurids are best known in the Late Jurassic of North America *(Brachiosaurus, "Supersaurus")* and East Africa *(Brachiosaurus)*, with some occurrences in the Early Cretaceous of Europe *(Pelorosaurus)*. The camarasaurids were also a Late Jurassic group from North America *(Camarasaurus)*, with possible relatives in the Cretaceous of Asia *(Euhelopus, Opisthocoelicaudia)*. The titanosaurids are restricted to the Late Cretaceous, and are known mainly from southern parts of the world: South America *(Antarctosaurus, Saltasaurus, Titanosaurus)* and India *(Titanosaurus)*. Finally, the diplodocids arose in the Late Jurassic of North America *(Apatosaurus, Barosaurus, Diplodocus)*, Africa *(Barosaurus, Dicraeosaurus)*, and Asia *(Mamenchisaurus)*.

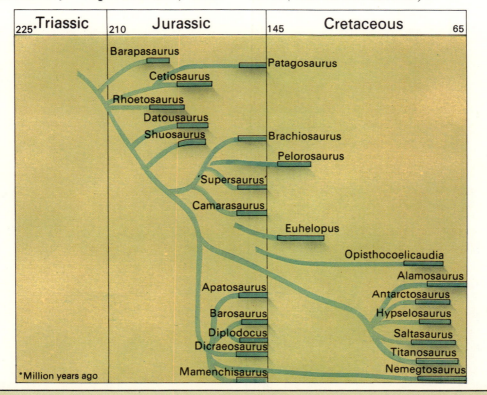

225.Triassic	210 Jurassic	145 Cretaceous 65

Barapasaurus
Patagosaurus
Cetiosaurus
Rhoetosaurus
Datousaurus
Shuosaurus
Brachiosaurus
Pelorosaurus
'Supersaurus'
Camarasaurus
Euhelopus
Opisthocoelicaudia
Alamosaurus
Apatosaurus
Antarctosaurus
Barosaurus
Hypselosaurus
Diplodocus
Saltasaurus
Dicraeosaurus
Titanosaurus
Nemegtosaurus
Mamenchisaurus

*Million years ago

SAUROPODOMORPHA

The suborder Sauropodomorpha is a division of the order Saurischia, the "lizard-hipped" dinosaurs. It includes two groups of medium and large plant-eating dinosaurs: the infraorder Prosauropoda (early plant-eating, or possibly plant- and meat-eating, animals with quite long necks), and the infraorder Sauropoda (later, large, four-legged plant eaters with long necks).

The Sauropodomorpha included the main plant-eating dinosaurs of the Late Triassic and the Jurassic. In the Early Jurassic, for example, there were four distinctive families of sauropodomorphs, and in the Late Jurassic, as many as four or five.

However, the sauropodomorphs declined in importance in the Cretaceous because of the rise of the ornithischian plant eaters. New groups such as the iguanodontids, ankylosaurs and stegosaurs rose to dominance in all parts of the world. By Late Cretaceous times, with the rise of the ceratopsians, pachycephalosaurs, and hadrosaurs, the sauropodomorphs had become very rare, with the exception of one or two late-surviving camarasaurids and diplodocids in Asia, and the titanosaurids.

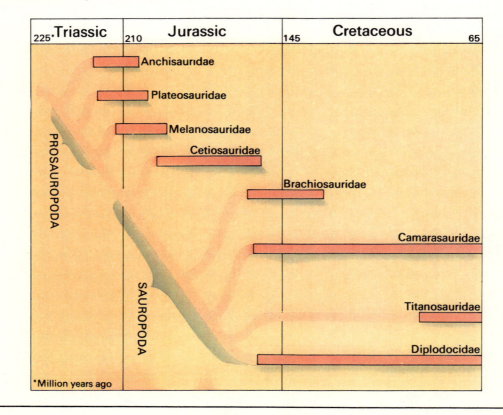

PROSAUROPODA

SAUROPODA

| 225·Triassic | 210 | Jurassic | 145 | Cretaceous | 65 |

Anchisauridae
Plateosauridae
Melanosauridae
Cetiosauridae
Brachiosauridae
Camarasauridae
Titanosauridae
Diplodocidae

*Million years ago

SAURORNITHOIDES

Saurornithoides
> sawr-OR-nith-OID-eez
? Bird-like reptile
(n) Dr. H. F. Osborn
    (1924)
(m) 28, 39

Cretaceous period

6ft.

Saurornithoides was an agile and intelligent, small meat eater. It had a long low head with small, sharp teeth, large eyes and a big brain for a reptile. The large brain allowed *Saurornithoides* to act and move quickly and to behave more intelligently than other dinosaurs. All that is known of *Saurornithoides* is the original specimen collected in 1923 on one of the American expeditions to the Gobi Desert in Mongolia. The remains consisted of most of a skull, parts of the backbone, hip region, and hind legs. More incomplete remains of *Saurornithoides* have been reported from Mongolia and North America. These include some jaw bones and teeth, but their identification has been very complicated. The Mongolian specimens are probably all forms of *Saurornithoides*, but the North American fossils are slightly different. Some of these have been named *Saurornithoides*, but others have been identified as a completely new form, *Pectinodon*. A new study of all the teeth and jaws has shown that the North American specimens actually belong to *Troodon*, and the Mongolian *Saurornithoides* may be *Troodon* too.

Saurornithoides skull (6 inches wide)

SCELIDOSAURUS

> skel-IDE-oh-SAW-rus
? Limb reptile
ⓝ Sir Richard Owen
  (1859)
ⓜ

Jurassic period

13ft.

Scelidosaurus was a strange, armored dinosaur. It was named from a collection of leg bones and a partial skull. It has now been shown that the leg bones come from a different animal—a megalosaur. Another good skeleton, including a skull, was described in 1863. This showed much of the skull, the armor, the legs, and the tail, but it lacked most of the arms and bones of the trunk. Some new skeletons of *Scelidosaurus* have been found recently, and these include material from the skull, the arms, and even the skin! *Scelidosaurus* had a small head with leaflike, ridged teeth. It had four strong legs and its body was armored with bony knobs and spikes.

Scelidosaurus has been difficult to fit into classifications of dinosaurs. It has been called an ornithopod, an ankylosaur, and a stegosaur by different scientists!

Scelidosaurus

SCUTELLOSAURUS

> skoot-EL-oh-SAW-rus
? Small-scaled reptile
ⓝ Dr. E. H. Colbert
  (1981)
ⓜ 19, 20

Jurassic period

50 inches

Scutellosaurus is an interesting early ornithopod that was named in 1981. It had a short skull with ridged plant-eating teeth. Its hind legs were longer than the arms, but by a smaller amount than in most ornithopods, and it probably walked on all fours or ran on its hind legs. *Scutellosaurus* had a very long tail—about one-and-a-half times its total length of 50 inches. It was armored, with hundreds of small bony knobs set in the skin of its back. This kind of armor has not been found in its relatives, such as *Fabrosaurus*.

Scutellosaurus shows evidence of two kinds of defensive strategy—it could run fast to escape from meat-eaters, or it could use its armor plates to protect itself.

Scutellosaurus

SECERNOSAURUS

> se-SER-no-SAW-rus
? Separate reptile
(n) Dr. M. Brett-Surman
(1979)
(m)

Cretaceous period

10ft.

Secernosaurus is the only duck-billed dinosaur known from South America. Most duckbills lived in North America and Asia, and this South American duckbill shows that there was a land connection which dinosaurs could cross. The name *Secernosaurus*, meaning "separate reptile," refers to the fact that it lived separate from its other relatives in the southern part of the world.

The fossils of *Secernosaurus* are very poor. They were collected in 1923 by an expedition to Argentina from the Field Museum in Chicago, and were not noticed in their collections for many years. They were first studied and named in 1979 when their geographic importance was realized. The remains consist of parts of the hip region, the shoulder blade, a bone from the lower leg, some tail bones, and part of the back of a skull. The hip bones show that *Secernosaurus* was a duckbill, and probably a small one, possibly as little as 10 feet long. The bones are most like those of *Edmontosaurus* and *Shantungosaurus*, and this shows that *Secernosaurus* almost certainly had a flat head, with no crest, just like those two forms. This shows how paleontologists can often make very good guesses about what certain dinosaurs might have looked like, even when they do not have all of the bones.

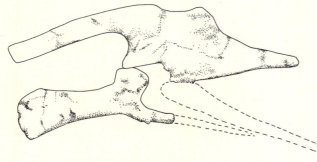

The hip bones from *Secernosaurus* viewed from the left-hand side (33 inches wide).

SEGISAURUS

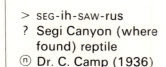

> SEG-ih-SAW-rus
? Segi Canyon (where found) reptile
ⓝ Dr. C. Camp (1936)
ⓜ

Cretaceous period

◄— 3ft. —►

Segisaurus is a curious, small dinosaur. The incomplete skeleton is rather like *Procompsognathus* in some features: the long, slim hind leg and foot are both similar. However, the bones of *Segisaurus* are solid, whereas animals like *Procompsognathus* and *Coelophysis* had hollow bones. Unfortunately, the skull and much of the backbone and arms are unknown. This means that it is difficult to decide exactly which were the closest relatives of *Segisaurus*. It was probably an active runner and meat-eater, but this is not certain. The poorly-preserved hand has sharp curved claws which suggests that *Segisaurus* may have captured and torn at the meat of small animals.

Segisaurus

SEGNOSAURIA

The infraorder Segnosauria was named in 1980 for some strange new dinosaurs that had been found in Mongolia. These were lightly built meat eaters with curious skulls. The most unusual feature was the hip which was not at all like a typical saurischian "lizard hip:" the two bones at the bottom both ran backward side-by-side, instead of one pointing forward and the other backward. All specimens of segnosaurs described so far come from Mongolia. They are very incomplete, and have been difficult to interpret. There are supposedly three segnosaurs, *Segnosaurus* itself, an animal called *Erlikosaurus*, and a third form, recently named *Enigmosaurus*.

The habits of *Segnosaurus* are hard to imagine. It was probably quite a slow-moving animal, which is odd for a meat-eater, and it might even have had webbed feet. The Russian scientists who named *Segnosaurus* said that it was possibly a swimming dinosaur which fed on fish. However, this is not very likely, since all other fish-eating animals, such as crocodiles, sharks, toothed whales, and the extinct sea-reptiles, had rows of long, pointed teeth at the front of the jaws. These allowed the animals to snatch rapidly-moving fish and hold them speared on their teeth so that they could not wriggle away. Any fish could have wriggled out of the front of the mouth of *Segnosaurus*—

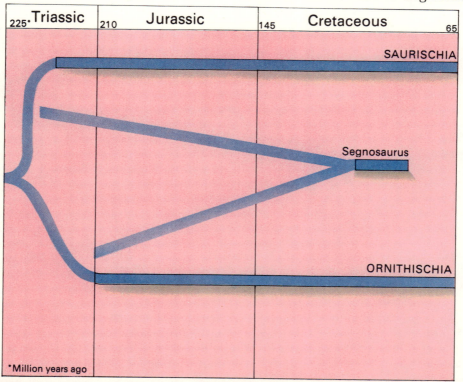

Triassic 225* | Jurassic 210 | Cretaceous 145 | 65

SAURISCHIA

Segnosaurus

ORNITHISCHIA

*Million years ago

its teeth were only at the back, near the jaw.

Erlikosaurus may be the same as *Segnosaurus*, but it was named as a new form in 1980 because it differed in a few ways. *Erlikosaurus* is known from a skull, part of the neck, an arm bone, and both feet. It was smaller than *Segnosaurus* and probably had teeth. The third segnosaur, named only in 1983, comes from the same area in Mongolia. It is a hip girdle, with the typical segnosaur characteristics.

The segnosaurids are generally said to be saurischians, and most likely theropods, because they were meat-eaters. (All other meat-eating dinosaurs are, of course, theropods.) It has been suggested recently that the segnosaurids lie somewhere in between the saurischians and the ornithischians.

Segnosaurus

SEGNOSAURUS

> SEG-no-saw-rus
? Slow reptile
(n) Drs. A. Perle & R. Barsbold (1979)
(m)

Cretaceous period

15ft.

Segnosaurus is known from a partial skeleton which includes a lower jaw, parts of the legs, arms, and backbone, and a complete hip girdle. The jaw has sharp, meat-cutting teeth at the back, but no teeth at all at the front. This area at the front might have been covered by a horny beak—a very strange arrangement for a meat-eater! The arms were short and the hands each had three fingers with sharp claws. Each foot had four toes.

The hip was unusual in shape in *Segnosaurus*, looking like that of an ornithischian rather than a saurischian dinosaur. The primitive three-pointed "lizard hip" became a two-pointed "bird hip." However, when studied in detail, it is clear that *Segnosaurus* is still a saurischian dinosaur, but it evolved the pattern of its hip bones separately from the ornithischians. The scientists who named *Segnosaurus* in 1979 suggested that it might have been a swimmer and that it fed on fish.

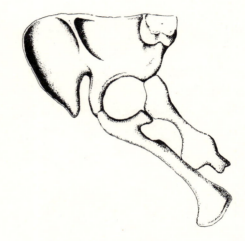

The hip bones from *Segnosaurus*

SHANTUNGOSAURUS

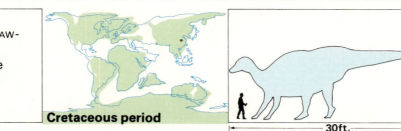

> shan-TUNG-oh-SAW-rus
? Shantung reptile
ⓝ C. C. Hu (1973)
ⓜ 38

Cretaceous period

30ft.

Shantungosaurus was an advanced, flat-headed, duck-billed dinosaur. It was the largest of this group, being over 30 feet long and 22 feet tall. It could have looked over the roof of a three-story house, and it must have weighed four or five times as much as its relatives. *Shantungosaurus* had a long, low skull with a flat duck-shaped beak and no crest. A nearly-complete skeleton of *Shantungosaurus* was discovered in the 1970s, and it is now on show in the Natural History Museum in Beijing, China. A grown man standing beside it just reaches the knee. Its closest relatives are *Edmontosaurus* and *Claosaurus* from North America, and *Secernosaurus* from South America, which shows how much the duck-billed dinosaurs must have migrated around the world in the Late Cretaceous.

Shantungosaurus

SHUNOSAURUS

> SHOO-no-SAW-rus
? Shu (where found) reptile
ⓝ Drs. Dong, Zhow & Chang (1983)
ⓜ 38

Jurassic period

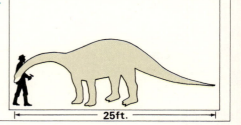

25ft.

The remains of the sauropod *Shunosaurus* were dug up in Sichuan Province of China in 1979. It seems to have been quite common in the Middle Jurassic of China, since more than ten skeletons have now been found, and these include some nearly complete remains. *Shunosaurus* was about 25 feet long, which is smaller than some of its relatives, such as *Barapasaurus*, *Cetiosaurus*, *Datousaurus*, *Patagosaurus*, and *Rhoetosaurus*. The head was quite large, and the jaws were lined with spoon-shaped teeth. The neck was shorter than in later sauropods, and the legs were massive.

Shunosaurus

SILVISAURUS

> SIL-vih-SAW-rus
? Forest reptile
ⓝ Dr. T. H. Eaton Jr (1960)
ⓜ

Cretaceous period

13ft

Silvisaurus was a medium-sized armored dinosaur. It was named in 1960 from a skull and partial skeleton which show that it was 13 feet long. The original specimen was found partly exposed in the bed of a stream where cattle went for water and it was damaged as a result of being trampled by the cattle. Another problem was that the bones were preserved in a very hard kind of rock, called ironstone, which took many hundreds of hours of work in the laboratory to remove.

Silvisaurus had a heavy head, quite a long neck, and a bulky body. It was unusual in having eight or nine small pointed teeth as well as a small horny beak near the front of the upper jaw. Other ankylosaurs did not have these front teeth, only the horn-covered beak. Its body was covered with an armor of flat, honeycomb-shaped or round plates. There were some rounded spikes sticking out sideways on the tail and part of the body. *Silvisaurus* was related to *Nodosaurus* and *Panoplosaurus*.

Silvisaurus

SPINOSAURUS

> SPINE-O-SAW-rus
? Spiny reptile
(n) Dr. E. Stromer (1915)
(m)

Cretaceous period

40ft.

Spinosaurus was a strange, meat-eating dinosaur with a sail on its back. The sail was made from skin and it was held up by tall spines on the back of each vertebra of the backbone. Some of these spines were more than 6 feet high—taller than a human being. *Spinosaurus* may have used its sail to control its body temperature: it could lose heat if it was too hot, or it could take in heat if it was too cold. Another idea is that the spines were covered with colorful skin and the sail might have been used for signaling to other dinosaurs.

The remains of *Spinosaurus* are rather incomplete. They consist of parts of the jaw and some parts of the backbone from the neck, back and tail. *Spinosaurus* had typical meat-eating teeth, like steak knives, but they were straight instead of curved. It was a giant animal, up to 40 feet long, and its closest relative may have been *Acrocanthosaurus*. It is interesting that one other dinosaur with a sail like that of *Spinosaurus* is *Ouranosaurus* which was found in the same part of North Africa.

Spinosaurus

STAURIKOSAURUS

> stor-ɪᴋ-oh-sᴀʏ-rus
? Cross reptile
ⓝ Dr. E. H. Colbert (1970)
ⓜ 19

Triassic period

6ft.

Staurikosaurus was an early two-legged dinosaur. It was 6 feet long and had a light, agile body. Its head was quite large and its teeth show that it probably ate meat. *Staurikosaurus* had long hind legs and shorter arms, all with five toes or fingers—which is a primitive feature. *Staurikosaurus* may have been related to early prosauropods or early coelurosaurs.

Staurikosaurus

STEGOCERAS

> steg-o-ser-as
? Horny roof
ⓝ Dr L. M. Lambe (1902)
ⓜ

Cretaceous period

7ft.

Stegoceras was a medium-sized plant-eater, 7 feet long, with a curious, thick skull. It was named in 1902 on the basis of two skull fragments which were thought at first to belong to a horned ceratopsian dinosaur. However, in the 1920s, a more complete skull and a partial skeleton were discovered, and these showed that *Stegoceras* belonged to a completely new group, now called the Pachycephalosauria. *Stegoceras* had a heavy skull covered with horny lumps and knobs. The top of the skull was very thick and it formed a high crest. This crest grew higher as *Stegoceras* grew older.

STEGOSAURIA

The suborder Stegosauria includes a selection of medium- and large-sized plant-eating dinosaurs. They all had an armor of spikes or plates, or both, along the middle of the back. Some also had spikes on their hips. There were two groups, the early scelidosaurids (which could be stegosaurs or ankylosaurs) and the later stegosaurids.

If *Scelidosaurus* is a stegosaur, then the group arose in Europe in the Early Jurassic. Not only are there now several specimens of *Scelidosaurus* from England, but also

a possible relative from Portugal. The true stegosaurs, the stegosaurids, arose in the Middle Jurassic of Europe *(Dacentrurus, Lexovisaurus)*, and then spread to Africa *(Kentrosaurus)* and North America *(Stegosaurus)* in the Late Jurassic. Possible stegosaurs are known from the Early Cretaceous of Europe and China, but the strangest feature of their history is that one form *(Dravidosaurus)* lived on to the end of the Late Cretaceous in India, long after the group had died out in all other parts of the world.

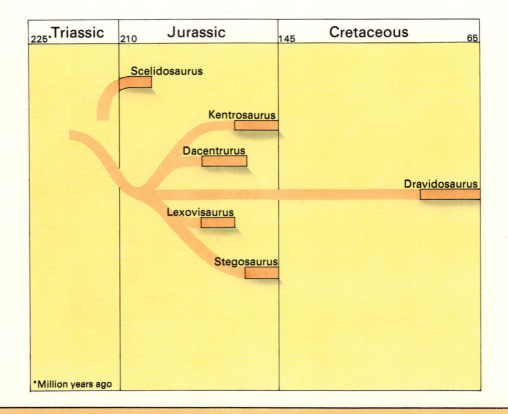

225 *Triassic   210   Jurassic   145   Cretaceous   65*

Scelidosaurus

Kentrosaurus

Dacentrurus

Dravidosaurus

Lexovisaurus

Stegosaurus

*Million years ago

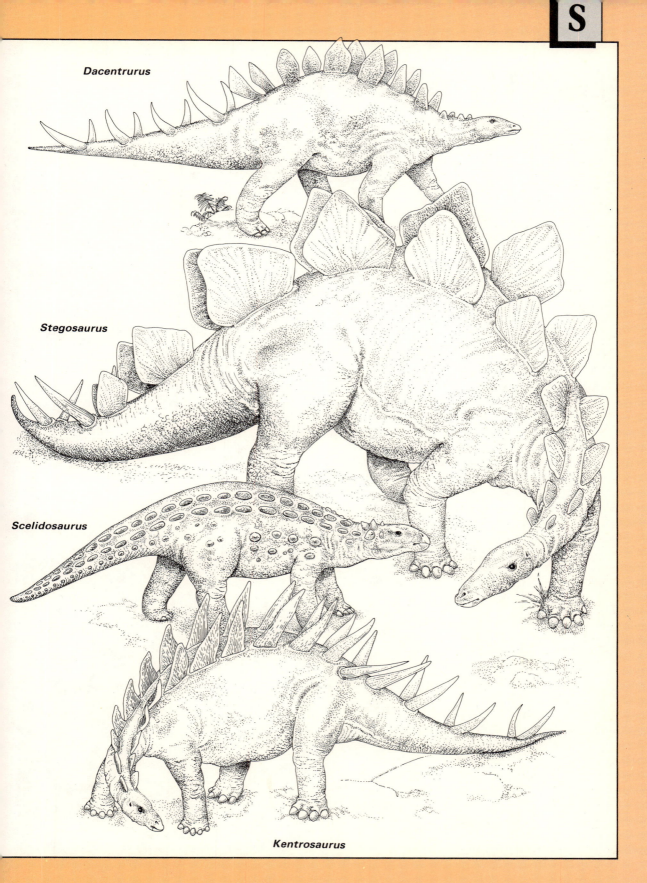

Dacentrurus

Stegosaurus

Scelidosaurus

Kentrosaurus

STEGOSAURUS

> STEG-oh-SAW-rus
? Roofed reptile
(n) Dr. O. C. Marsh (1877)
(m) 7, 9, 10, 11, 25, 30, 33, 35

Jurassic period

20–30ft.

Stegosaurus was named in 1877 from an incomplete skeleton from Colorado. *Stegosaurus* had a tiny tubular skull with a brain the size of a walnut. Its teeth were small, blunt and leaflike, and set in the back of the jaw. The front of the jaw was toothless. *Stegosaurus* had small, flat plates on its neck and bigger, diamond-shaped plates on its back and the first part of its tail. These plates are usually shown in two rows, but it has been suggested recently that there was only a single row, or even that they stuck out sideways like a protective shield over the back. At the end of the tail, *Stegosaurus* had four long spines. *Stegosaurus* had very short front legs, half the length of its hind legs. It was up to 30 feet long.

Stegosaurus

STENONYCHOSAURUS

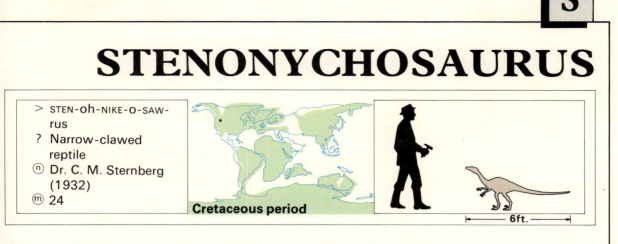

> STEN-**oh**-NIKE-O-SAW-rus
? Narrow-clawed reptile
Ⓝ Dr. C. M. Sternberg (1932)
Ⓜ 24

Cretaceous period

6ft.

Stenonychosaurus was probably the most intelligent dinosaur. It was a very lightly-built animal, about 6 feet long, with slender legs and a long tail. It had fairly long arms with thin fingers. *Stenonychosaurus* was an agile and fast-moving meat eater.

The original remains included a few vertebrae, some hand bones, and a complete foot. The foot had one very short, spurlike toe, and three main ones that were used for walking, like a bird's foot. The middle toe was shorter than the two side ones, and it bore a large claw. There were special joints in this toe so that the claw could be swung up and down, just like *Deinonychus*, for slashing at other dinosaurs. The most interesting feature of *Stenonychosaurus* is its head. It had very large eyes and a large brain, equivalent to a bird of the same size. *Stenonychosaurus* was an active, intelligent hunter with good senses and quick reflexes.

Stenonychosaurus

STRUTHIOMIMUS

> STROOTH-ee-oh-MIME-us

? Ostrich mimic

ⓝ Dr. H..F. Osborn (1917)

ⓜ

Cretaceous period

⟵ 12ft. ⟶

Struthiomimus was shaped just like an ostrich, but without feathers. It was 12 feet long and had a very slender body. The first specimen to be described in 1917 was more or less complete, and it lacked only part of the head, some parts of the backbone, and a few bones of the arms and legs. Its head was small and it had no teeth—only a horny beak. The skull was light, being made of very thin bones. It is likely that the skull was flexible and had some extra joints just as in modern birds. The beak portion of the skull could probably have been tilted up and down, and this might have allowed them to remove shells from nuts or fruits. *Struthiomimus* had a long neck and a long tail which was used for balance.

In many ways, *Struthiomimus* was rather birdlike, and especially like the living ostrich and other flightless birds of that type. The small head, long neck, and powerful legs are just the same, although the long tail and clawed hands of *Struthiomimus* are not a feature of modern birds. *Struthiomimus* could have used its three-fingered hands to dig up food and to grasp things.

Struthiomimus

STRUTHIOSAURUS

> STROOTH-ee-oh-SAW-rus
? Ostrich reptile
ⓝ Dr. E. Bunzel (1871)
ⓜ 58

Cretaceous period

6ft.

Struthiosaurus was the smallest known armored dinosaur. At only 6 feet long, it was less than half the size of its relatives *Acanthopholis*, *Hylaeosaurus*, and *Nodosaurus*. *Struthiosaurus* was also one of the last surviving ankylosaurs and is unusual in that it comes from Europe, rather than North America or Asia. Fossils of *Struthiosaurus* have been found in France, Hungary, and Austria, and especially in the Transylvania region of Romania (more famous as the home of the bloodthirsty Count Dracula!).

It is an odd fact that all Transylvanian dinosaurs are very small. Fossil discoveries there include a sauropod, a duckbill, and an iguanodontid ornithopod, as well as *Struthiosaurus*. It has been suggested that, in the Late Cretaceous, southern Europe consisted of a number of islands, and that this is why some dinosaurs were unusually small. Today, animals on islands are often smaller than their relatives on the mainland: for example the island of Madagascar has a dwarf hippopotamus, and some islands in the Mediterranean used to have dwarf elephants!

Struthiosaurus had a small head and five different kinds of bony armor: plates with a big spine and small bones on the neck, a pair of very long spines on the shoulders, pairs of sloping plates on the hips and tail, and smaller spines and knobs on the sides of the body and tail.

Armor plates from the skin of *Struthiosaurus* (left), and a bony spine (right) (both 7 inches long).

STYRACOSAURUS

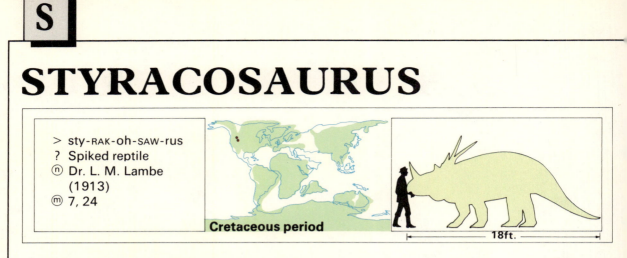

> sty-RAK-oh-SAW-rus
? Spiked reptile
ⓝ Dr. L. M. Lambe (1913)
ⓜ 7, 24

Cretaceous period

18ft.

Styracosaurus is a well-known horned dinosaur with a remarkable spiny frill. *Styracosaurus* was 18 feet long and it was probably related to *Monoclonius*. The skull was long and it had six long spines that pointed back over the neck. These six spines were formed from the lumps of bone that ran around the back of the frill in all other ceratopsians, but were usually only small and round, rather than long and pointed as in *Styracosaurus*. It also had a tall horn on its nose which pointed straight upward. There were two much smaller horns above the eyes. This formidable array would have helped *Styracosaurus* to protect itself against predators and might also have warned off rivals of the same species.

Styracosaurus

"SUPERSAURUS"

> super-SAW-rus
? Super reptile
(n) found Jim Jensen (1972)
(m) 6, 12

Jurassic period

80–100ft.

"*Supersaurus*" has not yet been properly named, but it may have been one of the largest dinosaurs known. The bones of "*Supersaurus*" were discovered in 1972, and they clearly belonged to an animal like *Brachiosaurus*. However, they were much bigger. There is no complete skeleton of "*Supersaurus*," only a few bones. These came from a single quarry in Colorado, which was located first by some amateur rock collectors. In 1971 they showed some smaller specimens to Jim Jensen, a famous bone collector, and he started digging in 1972. He expected to find some big dinosaurs, but did not expect the huge bones that were turned up. Jensen himself is quite tall, about 6 feet 2 inches, but the shoulder blade of "*Supersaurus*" was much longer than he when he lay down beside it. One of the neck bones was over 5 feet long. It has been estimated that "*Supersaurus*" was 80–100 feet long, and 50 feet high when it raised its neck; that is, as tall as a five-story building. An even bigger animal, known as "*Ultrasaurus*" was found in the same dinosaur beds in 1979.

The "*Supersaurus*" shoulder blade is taller than a man.

SYNTARSUS

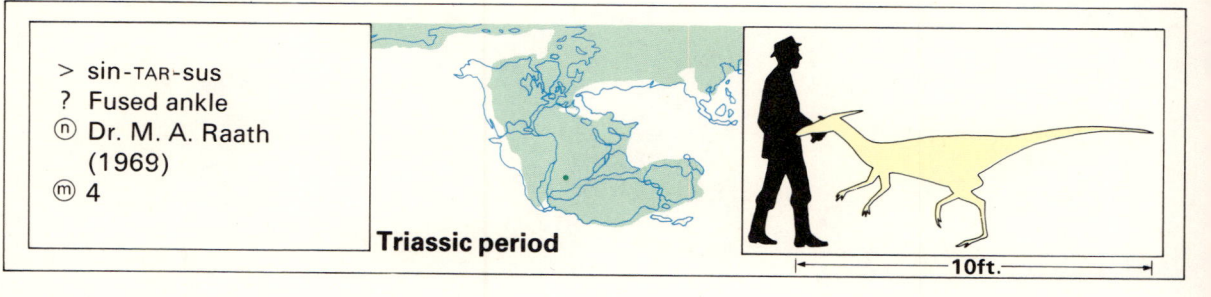

> sin-TAR-sus
? Fused ankle
ⓝ Dr. M. A. Raath (1969)
ⓜ 4

Triassic period

10ft.

Syntarsus is an interesting, small dinosaur. It was a lightly built, two-legged meat eater, 10 feet long, which is known from an incomplete skeleton from Zimbabwe. *Syntarsus* was rather like *Coelophysis* except that some of its ankle bones were fused or joined together. It had long powerful legs and short arms with three fingers, each of which had a powerful curved claw. Some scientists have reconstructed *Syntarsus* with a plume on the back of its head and a covering of feathers. This was because they wanted to prove that dinosaurs were warm-blooded like birds. However, there is no evidence that *Syntarsus* had feathers.

Syntarsus

TARBOSAURUS

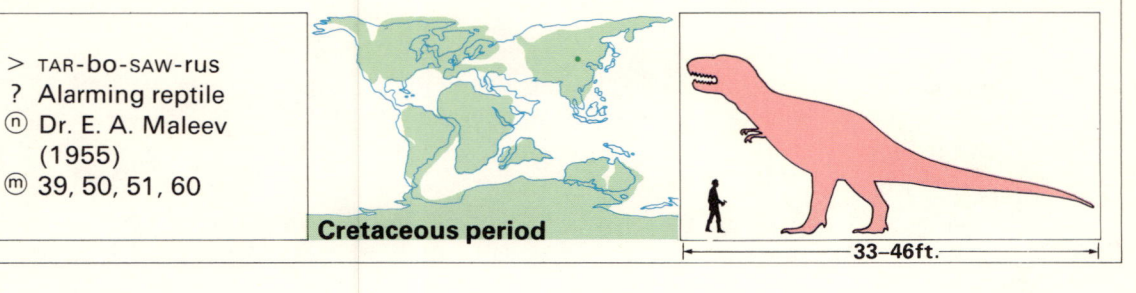

> TAR-bo-SAW-rus
? Alarming reptile
Ⓝ Dr. E. A. Maleev (1955)
Ⓜ 39, 50, 51, 60

Cretaceous period

33–46ft.

Tarbosaurus was a large meat eater, an Asian relative of *Tyrannosaurus*. It was about the same size as *Tyrannosaurus*, but less heavily built. It was named in 1955 on the basis of seven skeletons collected on a Russian expedition to the Gobi Desert, Mongolia. Six more skeletons were found later, on a joint Polish-Mongolian trip. *Tarbosaurus* had a longer skull than *Tyrannosaurus*, and 27 large, curved, knife-like teeth along its upper jaw. The jaws were deep, with large muscles which were attached near the back. These gave a powerful bone-crushing bite.

Tarbosaurus had very short arms with only two fingers on each hand.

The two fingers are numbers one and two (equivalent to the "thumb" and the "index finger"). Two of the other five fingers have been lost completely, and the middle finger is reduced to a tiny stump. It is hard to see what these reduced hands were used for, since they could not even reach the mouth. The feet were birdlike. There were three main toes which pointed forward and reached the ground. The fourth toe was small, and it pointed backward. *Tarbosaurus* was 33 to 46 feet long, and it could have fed on the duck-billed dinosaurs and armored dinosaurs that lived with it in Mongolia.

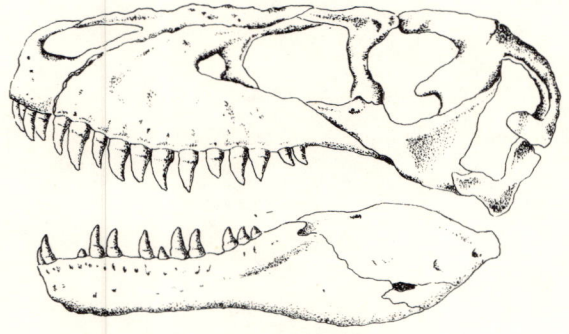

Tarbosaurus skull (5 feet wide)

THECODONTOSAURUS

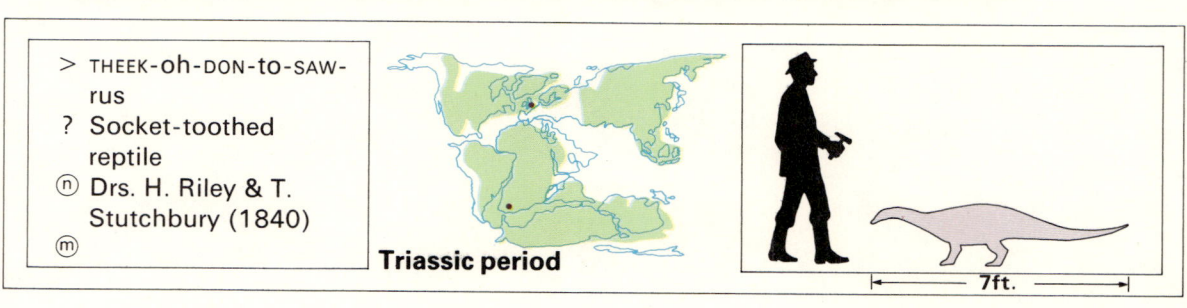

> THEEK-oh-DON-to-SAW-rus

? Socket-toothed reptile

(n) Drs. H. Riley & T. Stutchbury (1840)

(m)

Triassic period

7ft.

Thecodontosaurus was an early, medium-sized dinosaur. It was named in 1840 from a piece of jaw found in Bristol, southwest England. Other early discoveries included a number of teeth, jaw bones, bones from the backbone, ribs, and odd bones from the arms and legs. Since the 1840s, many more partial skeletons and skulls of *Thecodontosaurus* have been found in southwestern England, nearly all in ancient caves or fissures. It seems that these small dinosaurs were walking around on a limestone surface in the Late Triassic, and some of them fell into cracks in the rock. These cracks were then filled with Triassic muds and sands, and the bodies of small animals became trapped. Some bones of a moderate-sized prosauropod from South Africa were later named *Thecodontosaurus*, but these have now been shown to belong to *Anchisaurus*.

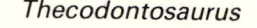

Thecodontosaurus

THERIZINOSAURUS

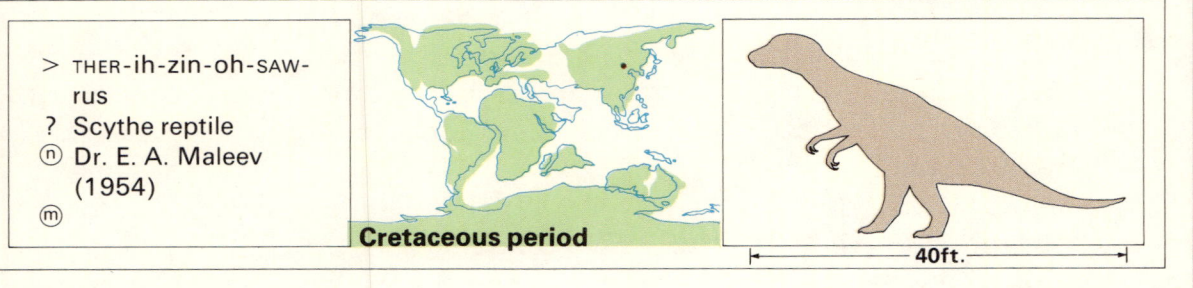

> THER-ih-zin-oh-SAW-
rus
? Scythe reptile
ⓝ Dr. E. A. Maleev
(1954)
ⓜ

Cretaceous period

40ft.

Therizinosaurus was the name recently given to a huge arm with fierce claws found in Mongolia. The arm was about 8 feet long in all, and its single scythe-like claw was 27 inches around its outer curve. This length does not include the horny covering that would have enclosed the claw, and might have made the whole claw as much as 3 feet long! That makes the claw alone the size of a hand-held scythe used for cutting long grass, but the *Therizinosaurus*

claw was much heavier. The first specimens were some very large claws found on the joint Soviet-Mongolian expedition in 1948, and in later trips in 1957, 1959 and 1960 to the Gobi Desert and other parts of Mongolia. Associated fossils included incomplete legs and a tooth. *Therizinosaurus* may be related to *Deinocheirus*, or to the deinonychosaurs, but this is very uncertain.

An arm from *Therizinosaurus*, seen from the left-hand side. A different view of the claw is seen above. Measured around the curve it is 27 inches long.

THEROPODA

The suborder Theropoda includes all of the small-, medium- and large-sized meat-eating dinosaurs. There were five main groups: the coelurosaurs (small and medium-sized, lightly built), the ornithomimosaurs (very slender, ostrich-like), the deinonychosaurs (lightly built, large fierce claws), the segnosaurs (with an unusual hip), and the carnosaurs (all the heavy medium and large forms).

The coelurosaurs are a broad group of small meat eaters that include some of the first dinosaurs from the Late Triassic, and later ones from the Jurassic and Cretaceous. It is difficult to study the evolution of the coelurosaurs but it is thought that they gave rise to the other meat eaters—the carnosaurs in the Early Jurassic, the ornithomimosaurs in the Late Jurassic, and the deinonychosaurs and segnosaurs (possibly) in the Early Cretaceous. The theropods include one other group that became even more important than any of those just mentioned—the birds. The oldest birds, called *Archaeopteryx* ("ancient wing") are known from the Late Jurassic of Germany. Their feathers are beautifully preserved in limy mudrock, and their skeletons are very like those of small dinosaurs. It is now thought that the birds share their closest common ancestor with deinonychosaurs.

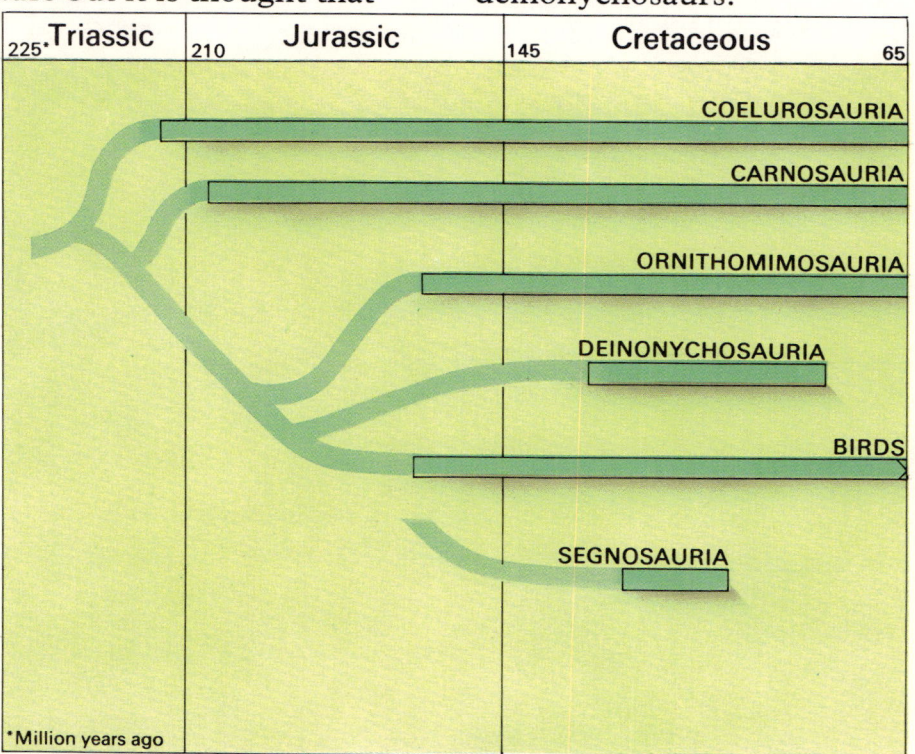

225 Triassic	210 Jurassic	145 Cretaceous 65

COELUROSAURIA

CARNOSAURIA

ORNITHOMIMOSAURIA

DEINONYCHOSAURIA

BIRDS

SEGNOSAURIA

*Million years ago

TITANOSAURUS

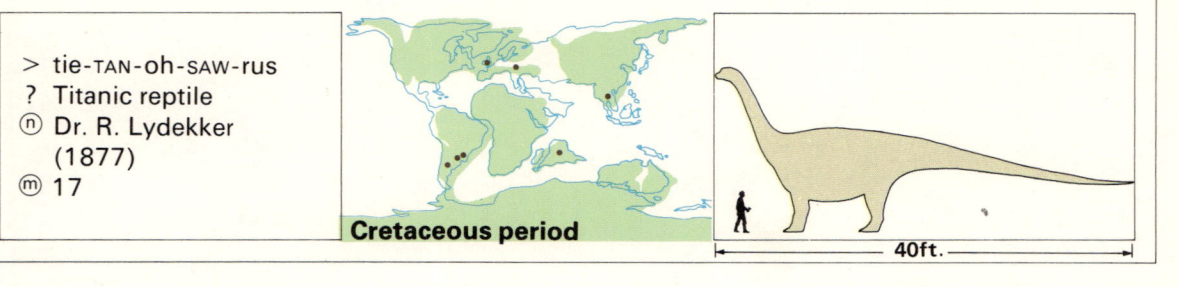

> tie-TAN-oh-SAW-rus
? Titanic reptile
ⓝ Dr. R. Lydekker (1877)
ⓜ 17

Cretaceous period

40ft.

Titanosaurus was a medium-sized sauropod. Ten or more species of *Titanosaurus* have been named from countries as far apart as India, Hungary, and Argentina. The fact that this one dinosaur has been found in so many parts of the world shows that it was able to migrate freely. *Titanosaurus* was about 40 feet long and rather heavily built. It had a long tail, a shorter neck, and a broad back probably covered with armor, as in *Saltasaurus*.

The first specimens of *Titanosaurus* were found in India. The dinosaur was in fact named from a few tail vertebrae and a thigh bone found 100 years ago. About 50 years later some more leg bones of the same animal were found in India. Other species of *Titanosaurus* were named from Argentina, but scientists have suggested recently that these might actually belong to *Saltasaurus*. Unfortunately, no skull from *Titanosaurus* has been discovered, other than an incomplete braincase, and this makes it difficult to decide what the habits of this dinosaur were, and to which dinosaurs it was related.

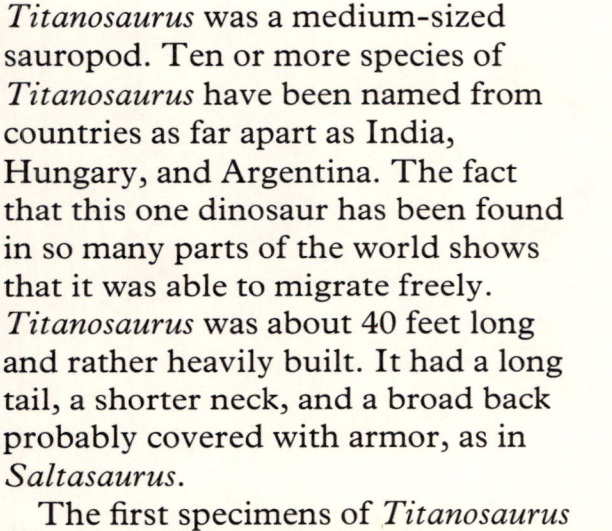

Titanosaurus shoulder girdle (above) (24 inches long) and upper arm bone (22 inches long).

TOROSAURUS

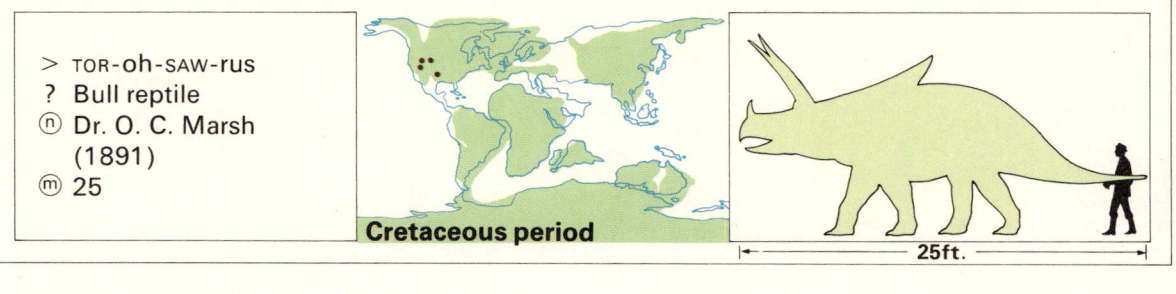

> TOR-oh-SAW-rus
? Bull reptile
ⓝ Dr. O. C. Marsh (1891)
ⓜ 25

Cretaceous period

25ft.

Torosaurus had the longest, bony neck frill of all the horned dinosaurs. It is known only from two skulls, each of which has been named as a separate species of *Torosaurus*. One of these skulls has holes and irregular marks that show that this dinosaur had bone cancer. *Torosaurus* had a horny beak, a small horn on its nose, and two large horns pointing forward above its eyes. The frill at the back of the skull was longer than the skull itself. The frill was smoother in outline at the back than that of many other ceratopsians, and quite low. It also had small openings through the bone which reduced the weight, but these openings were smaller than in other similar dinosaurs. One specimen of *Torosaurus* is a skull that is 8 feet long: this is the biggest head of any known land animal. The head alone would have been the size of a small car. *Torosaurus* was about 25 feet long overall.

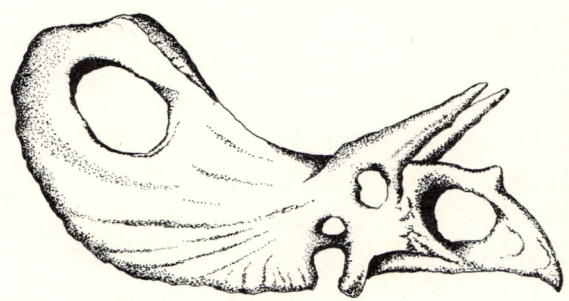

Torosaurus skull (5 feet wide)

TRICERATOPS

> try-SER-a-tops
? Three-horned face
ⁿ Dr. O. C. Marsh (1889)
ᵐ 7, 8, 24, 30, 44, 51, 57, 63, 65

Cretaceous period

30ft.

Triceratops is the best-known horned dinosaur. The first bones of *Triceratops* were probably collected by Edward Cope's bone collectors, but these were all too poor to identify from what sort of animal they came. Cope's great rival, Othniel C. Marsh *(see page 14)*, was the first to find a good enough specimen to describe, even if he wrongly identified it as a bison at first! He named *Triceratops* in 1889, and between 1889 and 1892, Marsh's collectors found 30 more skulls and skeletons. *Triceratops* is probably now the best-known ceratopsian. Since 1890, nearly 20 species of *Triceratops* have been named, some from very poor material.

Triceratops had three horns: one on its nose and two long ones above its eyes. Its neck frill was fairly short, and the back edge was surrounded by a zig-zag of knobs of bone. *Triceratops* was heavily built, with strong legs. Each finger or toe had a small hoof on the end. *Triceratops* was very large, measuring up to 30 feet long.

Triceratops

TROODON

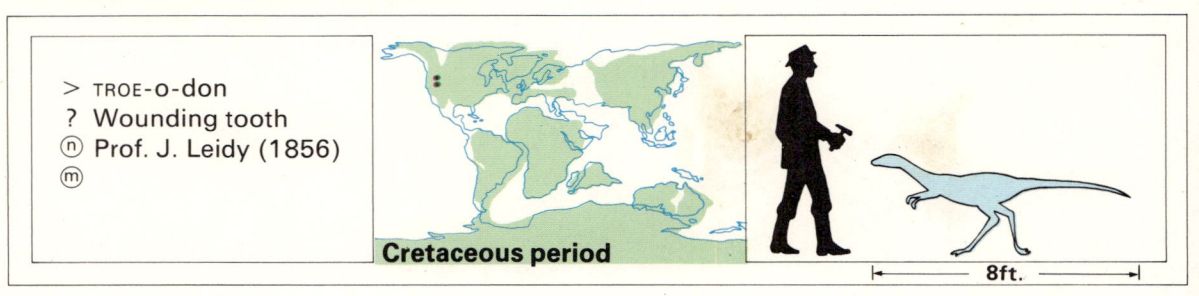

> TROE-o-don
? Wounding tooth
ⓝ Prof. J. Leidy (1856)
ⓜ

Cretaceous period

8ft.

Troodon is a poorly-known and very unusual animal. A pointed saw-edged tooth was named *Troodon* in 1856, and in the 1920s more discoveries seemed to show that it was the same as the bonehead *Stegoceras*. A skull of *Stegoceras* was found which had *Troodon*-like teeth at the front of the jaw. Some scientists argued that *Stegoceras* should be renamed *Troodon* since that name had been given first. However, since it was given to a single tooth alone, most people prefer to keep *Stegoceras* as a separate name. A recent study of the original specimens, published in 1987, has shown that the *Troodon* tooth is identical to the teeth of *Stenonychosaurus*. So, after a complex history, in which *Troodon* has been classified as a lizard, a megalosaurid dinosaur, a pachycephalosaur, and a hypsilophodontid, it turns out to be a saurornithoidid deinonychosaur—a lightly-built meat-eater that presumably had large slashing claws.

TSINTAOSAURUS

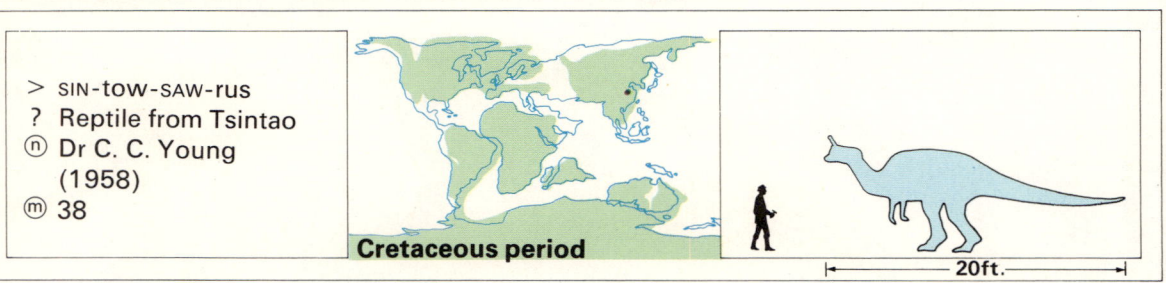

> SIN-tow-SAW-rus
? Reptile from Tsintao
ⓝ Dr C. C. Young (1958)
ⓜ 38

Cretaceous period

20ft.

Tsintaosaurus was a strange duck-billed dinosaur. It had a tall horn on the top of its head just between the eyes. The horn pointed forward and it was hollow. The breathing tubes ran up inside the horn to the top, but there was no opening there.

Tsintaosaurus was large—between 20 and 33 feet long. It may be related to *Saurolophus* or to *Parasaurolophus*.

TYRANNOSAURUS

> tie-RAN-oh-SAW-rus
? Tyrant reptile
ⓝ Prof. H. F. Osborn (1905)
ⓜ 7, 9, 10, 16, 32, 34, 57, 63

Cretaceous period

48ft.

Tyrannosaurus may be the best-known dinosaur. It was certainly one of the biggest meat eaters, and probably the most frightening that has ever lived. It was up to 48 feet long and 20 feet high: a man would hardly have reached its knee. Various odd teeth were found in the 19th century, but the first reasonably good skeleton was not found until 1902. This included parts of the skull and jaws, and odd bones from the backbone, shoulder, hip, and legs. A more complete skeleton was found in 1908, and this gave paleontologists more detailed information.

Tyrannosaurus had a massive head which was 5 feet long. The powerful jaws were lined with large, sharp teeth. Single teeth were up to 7 inches long, the size of a butcher's heavy chopping knife. *Tyrannosaurus* could probably swallow human beings whole if it was alive today.

Tyrannosaurus

'ULTRASAURUS'

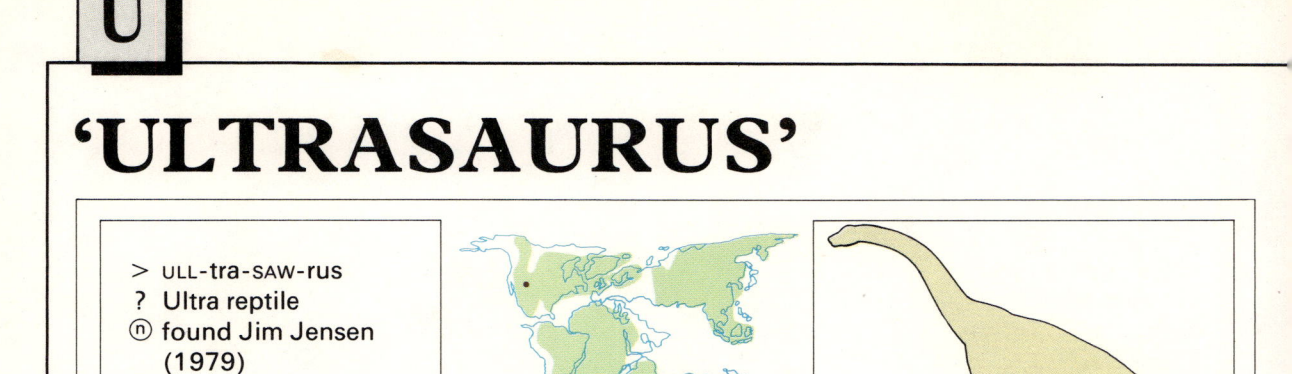

> ULL-tra-SAW-rus
? Ultra reptile
ⓝ found Jim Jensen (1979)
ⓜ 12

Jurassic period

100ft.

"*Ultrasaurus*" was discovered in 1979 in the same area of Colorado, which also produced "*Supersaurus.*" The remains are incomplete, but include a huge arm and shoulder girdle which indicate a height of about 26 feet at the shoulder—four times the height of a tall man! These remarkable new fossils have not yet been properly described or named. "*Ultrasaurus*" was probably even bigger than "*Supersaurus*" measuring up to 100 feet long. Like "*Supersaurus,*" it was a relative of *Brachiosaurus*; this can be worked out on the basis of the few bones that have been found so far. It has been estimated that, if *Brachiosaurus* weighed about 70 tons, then "*Ultrasaurus*" might have reached as much as 130 tons! This was the largest land animal that ever lived, and it is only approached in weight by the giant blue whale which can weigh up to 100 tons.

The tallest dinosaurs:
"*Ultrasaurus*" (1),
"*Supersaurus*" (2) and
Brachiosaurus (3).

1
2
3

VELOCIRAPTOR

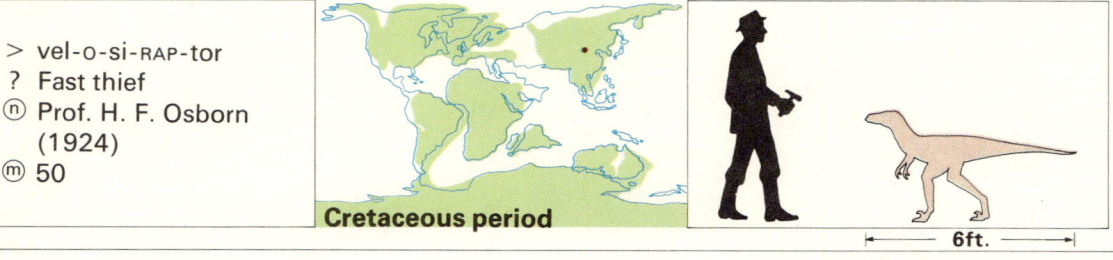

> vel-o-si-RAP-tor
? Fast thief
ⓝ Prof. H. F. Osborn (1924)
ⓜ 50

Cretaceous period

6ft.

Velociraptor was a medium-sized, lightly built meat eater. It had a long low skull, with a very flat snout and no more than 30 pointed, curved teeth in its jaw, while relatives such as *Saurornithoides* had rather more. The shape of the head, being very long and low, clearly sets it apart from other deinonychosaurs. One toe of each foot was large and bore a scythe-like claw.

The original specimens of *Velociraptor* were collected in the early 1920s by an American expedition to the Gobi Desert in Mongolia. It was not clear what kind of dinosaur *Velociraptor* was until the discovery of *Deinonychus* in the 1960s

which showed the powerful jaws and great hunting claw on the foot in detail. In 1971 a specimen of *Velociraptor* was found which had died while attacking a *Protoceratops*. *Velociraptor* had a firm hold of the head-shield of *Protoceratops* and was kicking at the belly of *Protoceratops* with its huge foot-claw. *Protoceratops* had pierced the chest region of *Velociraptor* with its armored head. They must have killed each other at exactly the same time.

Velociraptor

VULCANODON

> vul-KAN-oh-don
? Volcano tooth
ⓝ Prof. M. A. Raath
(1972)
ⓜ 4

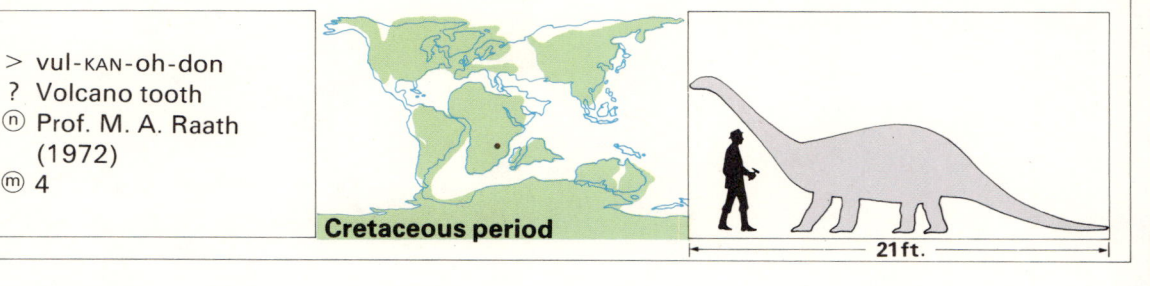

Cretaceous period

21 ft.

Vulcanodon is a strange animal that was named in 1972. Only part of the skeleton is known—nearly everything except the neck and head was found. The name *Vulcanodon* refers to some small teeth with serrated edges found with it, but these probably came from a meat-eater. The hips of *Vulcanodon* were like those of a prosauropod while its limbs were like those of a sauropod, so that it is probably a kind of "missing link" between the prosauropods and the sauropods.

Vulcanodon could be related to *Melanorosaurus* or to *Cetiosaurus*. *Vulcanodon* was about 21 feet long.

Vulcanodon

XIAOSAURUS

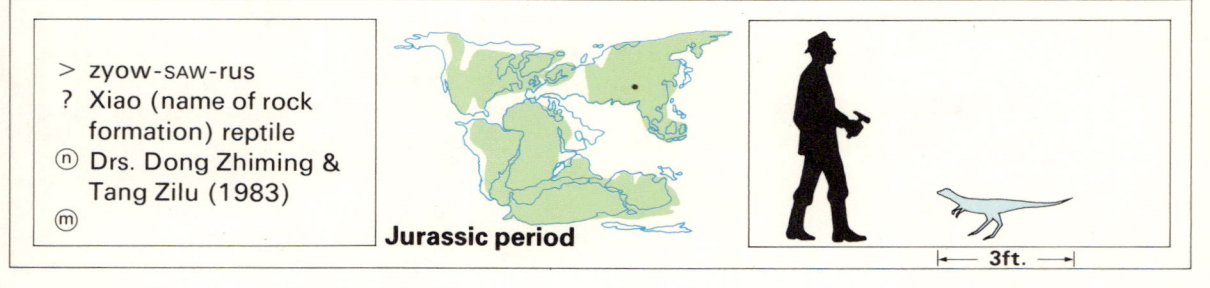

> zyow-SAW-rus
> ? Xiao (name of rock formation) reptile
> (n) Drs. Dong Zhiming & Tang Zilu (1983)
> (m)

Jurassic period

3ft.

Xiaosaurus was a small, fabrosaurid plant eater which was found in Sichuan Province, China. It is known from a partial jaw and a leg, and these are most like *Fabrosaurus*.

XUANHANOSAURUS

> zwan-HAN-o-SAW-rus
> ? Xuanhan (where found) reptile
> (n) Dr. Dong Zhiming (1984)
> (m)

Jurassic period

20ft.

Xuanhanosaurus is a poorly-known, megalosaurid meat eater from the Middle Jurassic of Sichuan Province, China. It is known only from two bones of the backbone, a shoulder girdle, and parts of an arm and a hand. These are most like the shoulder and arm bones of *Allosaurus* and *Megalosaurus*.

ZEPHYROSAURUS

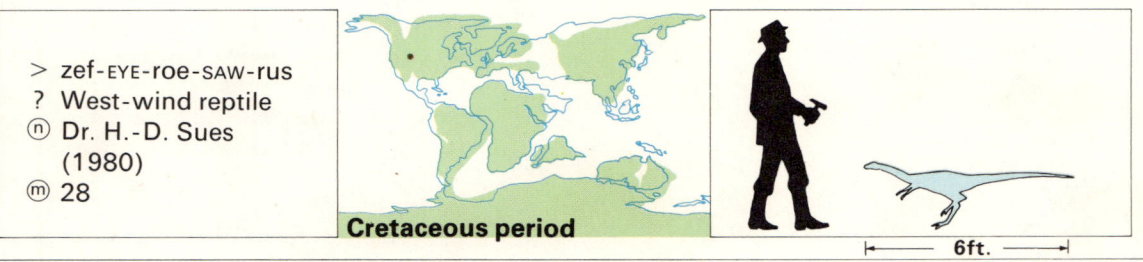

> zef-EYE-roe-SAW-rus
> ? West-wind reptile
> (n) Dr. H.-D. Sues (1980)
> (m) 28

Cretaceous period

6ft.

Zephyrosaurus was rather like *Hypsilophodon*. It was named in 1980 from a skull and a few vertebrae.

Zephyrosaurus had small, ridged teeth which were adapted for efficient chopping of plant food.

DIRECTORY OF MUSEUMS

This is a worldwide directory of many of the museums in which you can see dinosaur displays. To find out where you can see a certain dinosaur, turn to the guide section *(pages 18–165)* and find the line marked ⓜ.

The numbers listed there correspond to the numbered museums in this directory. If there are no numbers listed, then this particular dinosaur cannot be seen in any of the museums listed here.

AFRICA

1. **Bernard Price Institute of Palaeontology**, Johannesburg, South Africa.
2. **Musée National du Niger**, Niamey, Niger
3. **Museum of Earth Sciences**, Rabat, Morocco.
4. **National Museum of Zimbabwe**, Harare, Zimbabwe.
5. **South African Museum**, Cape Town, South Africa.

NORTH AND SOUTH AMERICA

6. **Academy of Natural Sciences**, Philadelphia, Pennsylvania.
7. **American Museum of Natural History**, New York, New York.
8. **Buffalo Museum of Science**, Buffalo, New York.
9. **Carnegie Museum of Natural History**, Pittsburgh, Pennsylvania.
10. **Denver Museum of Natural History**, Denver, Colorado.
11. **Dinosaur National Monument**, Jensen, Utah.
12. **Earth Sciences Museum** (Brigham Young University), Provo, Utah.
13. **Field Museum of Natural History**, Chicago, Illinois.
14. **Fort Worth Museum of Science**, Fort Worth, Texas.
15. **Houston Museum of Natural Science**, Houston, Texas.
16. **Los Angeles County Museum**, Los Angeles, California.
17. **Museo Argentino de Ciencias Naturales**, Buenos Aires, Argentina.
18. **Museum of La Plata University**, La Plata, Argentina.
19. **Museum of Comparative Zoology** (Harvard University), Cambridge, Massachusetts.
20. **Museum of Northern Arizona**, Flagstaff, Arizona.
21. **Museum of Paleontology** (University of California), Berkeley, California.
22. **Museum of the Rockies**, Bozeman, Montana.
23. **Natural History Museum**, Mexico City, Mexico.
24. **National Museum of Natural Sciences**, Ottawa, Canada.
25. **Peabody Museum of Natural History**, New Haven, Connecticut.
26. **Pratt Museum** (Amherst College), Amherst, Massachusetts.
27. **Provincial Museum of Alberta**, Edmonton, Canada.
28. **Redpath Museum**, Quebec, Canada.
29. **Royal Ontario Museum**, Toronto, Canada.
30. **Smithsonian Institution**, (National Museum of Natural History), Washington D.C.
31. **Stovall Museum**, Norman, Oklahoma.
32. **Tyrrell Museum of Palaeontology**, Drumheller, Canada.
33. **University of Michigan Exhibit Museum**, Ann Arbor, Michigan.
34. **University of Wyoming** (Geological Museum), Laramie, Wyoming.
35. **Utah Museum of Natural History** (University of Utah), Salt Lake City, Utah.

ASIA
36. **Beipei Museum**, Beipei, China.
37. **Indian Statistical Institute**, Calcutta, India.
38. **Institute of Vertebrate Paleontology and Paleoanthropology**, Beijing, China.
39. **Mongolian Academy of Sciences**, Ulan Bator, Mongolia.

AUSTRALIA

40. **Australian Museum**, Sydney, New South Wales.
41. **Queensland Museum**, Fortitude Valley, Queensland.

EUROPE

42. **Bavarian State Collection for Paleontology and Historical Geology**, Munich, West Germany.
43. **Bernissart Museum**, Hainaut, Belgium.
44. **Birmingham Museum**, Birmingham, United Kingdom.
45. **Central Geological Museum**, Leningrad, USSR.
46. **The Dinosaur Museum**, Dorchester, United Kingdom.
47. **Geological and Paleontological Institute** (University of Munster) Munster, West Germany.
48. **Humboldt University** (Natural History Museum), East Berlin, East Germany.
49. **Institute and Museum of Geology and Paleontology**, (University of Tubingen) Tubingen, West Germany.

50. **Institute of Paleobiology**, Warsaw, Poland.

A skeleton of *Brachiosaurus* in the Humboldt Museum, East Berlin, East Germany.

51. **Institut de Paléontologie**, Paris, France.
52. **Institut Royal des Sciences Naturelles de Belgique**, Brussels, Belgium.
53. **The Leicestershire Museum**, Leicester, United Kingdom.
54. **Musée Nationale d'Histoire Naturelle**, Paris, France.
55. **Museo Civico di Storia Naturale di Venezia**, Venice, Italy.
56. **Museum of Isle of Wight Geology**, Sandown, Isle of Wight, United Kingdom.
57. **Natural History Museum** (British Museum), London, United Kingdom.
58. **Natural History Museum**, Vienna, Austria.
59. **Oxford University Museum**, Oxford, United Kingdom.
60. **Paleontological Institute**, Moscow, USSR.
61. **Paleontological Museum** (Uppsala University), Uppsala, Sweden.
62. **Sedgwick Museum** (Cambridge University), Cambridge, United Kingdom.
63. **Senckenberg Nature Museum**, Frankfurt, West Germany.
64. **Stuttgart Museum**, Stuttgart, West Germany.
65. **Royal Scottish Museum**, Edinburgh, United Kingdom.

The giant duck-billed dinosaur *Shantungosaurus* in the Beijing Natural History Museum.

GLOSSARY

Ankylosaur ("stiff reptile") An armored dinosaur with a covering of bony plates on its back, and a knobby tail. *See* Ankylosauria in the guide.

Armored dinosaur There were three groups of armored dinosaurs which were protected by coverings of bony plates, spikes, or horns. *See* Ankylosauria, Ceratopsia, and Stegosauria in the guide.

Bacteria ("small stick") Simple, microscopic creatures that are made up from single cells.

Biologist ("life expert") A scientist who studies living plants and animals.

Braincase The part of the skull which contains the brain.

Carnosaur ("flesh-eating reptile") A large meat-eating dinosaur, such as *Tyrannosaurus* or *Allosaurus*. *See* Carnosauria in the guide.

Cell ("small space") The basic units which make up all living things.

Cenozoic ("recent life") The age of the mammals, from 65 million years ago to the present day.

Ceratopsian ("horned face") A plant-eating dinosaur with horns on its snout and face, and a horny frill over its neck. Examples are *Protoceratops* and *Triceratops*. *See* Ceratopsia in the guide.

Cheek teeth The teeth at the back of the jaw which may be used for grinding up food.

Classification The sorting of animals and plants into an order that shows how they are related to each other.

Coelurosaur ("hollow reptile") A small meat-eating dinosaur, such as *Coelophysis* or *Compsognathus*. *See* Coelurosauria in the guide.

Cranium The bones that cover the top of the head or skull roof.

Continental drift The movement of the land masses on Earth over millions of years.

Cretaceous ("chalk age") The third geological period in the "age of the dinosaurs," the time from 144 to 65 million years ago. Vast layers of chalk were deposited during the Late Cretaceous hence the name "chalk age".

Deinonychosaur ("terrible-clawed reptile") A meat-eating dinosaur which lived in Cretaceous times. Deinonychosaurs had large scythe-like claws on their hind feet with which they attacked their prey. *See* Deinonychosauria in the guide.

Deposit ("laid down") A mass of sedimentary rocks, such as mudstones and sandstones.

Duck-billed dinosaur Another name for a hadrosaur, a kind of two-legged plant eater that had a broad beaklike snout.

Era A long period of geological time, such as the Mesozoic era.

Evolution ("unfolding") The development of plants and animals through geological time, and the way that this development has come about. Animals and plants evolve, or develop, as a result of changes in their living conditions.

Evolutionary tree The pattern of evolution, showing how different plants or animals are related. This looks like a tree since it starts with one species which then evolves and splits into many branches.

Extinction ("wiping out") The death of a group of plants or animals.

Family A group of closely related plants or animals.

Fossil ("dug up") The remains of something that once lived. Fossils are often millions of years old, and turned to stone.

Genus A group of very closely related species of plants or animals. We say one *genus*, two *genera*.

Geologist ("earth-expert") A scientist who studies rocks and the history of the Earth.

Hadrosaur ("big reptile") A plant-eating dinosaur of the Late Cretaceous, often known as a "duck-billed" dinosaur because of its broad flat snout.

Infraorder ("below order") A division of an order of plants or animals. The infraorder Carnosauria is a subgroup of the order Saurischia.

Jurassic ("Jura age": from the Jura mountains where rocks from this period were first named) The second geological period of the "age of the dinosaurs;" the time from 208 to 144 million years ago.

Mammal A warm-blooded animal with hair, that produces milk to feed its young. Examples are mice, rabbits, elephants, and humans.

Mesozoic ("middle age") The "age of the dinosaurs," the time from 245 to 65 million years ago which includes the Triassic, Jurassic, and Cretaceous periods. The Mesozoic is the "middle age" between the Paleozoic and Cenozoic eras.

Migration ("moving") The movement of large groups of animals over large distances. For example, during winter many birds migrate south to warmer climates.

Mudstone A fine-grained sedimentary rock formed from hardened mud.

Order A large group of species that are rather distantly related to each other—a larger group than a genus or family.

Ornithischian ("bird hip") This order of dinosaurs includes all of the two-legged plant eaters, and all of the armored dinosaurs. *See* Ornithischia in the guide.

Ornithomimosaur ("bird-mimic reptile") A two-legged slender meat-eater, such as *Ornithomimus*. *See* Ornithomimosauria in the guide.

Ornithopod ("bird-foot") A plant-eating dinosaur that had no spines or horns and walked on two legs. Examples include *Iguanodon* and the duck-billed dinosaurs. *See* Ornithopoda in the guide.

Pachycephalosaur ("thick-headed reptile") A plant-eating dinosaur with a very thick skull roof, possibly used for head-butting. *See* Pachycephalosauria in the guide.

Paleontologist ("expert on ancient life") A scientist who studies fossils and the history of life.

Paleozoic ("ancient life") The first era of common life, lasting from 570 to 245 million years ago. The "age of fishes and amphibians."

Period A division of geological time, such as the Triassic, Jurassic, or the Cretaceous.

Phanerozoic ("common life") The time interval from 570 million years ago to the present day, when fossils are commonly found. The Phanerozoic is divided into the Palaeozoic, Mesozoic, and Cenozoic eras.

Precambrian ("before Cambrian") The first division of time on Earth, from the origin of the Earth, 4.6 billion years ago, to the beginning of the Phanerozoic, 570 million years ago.

Prosauropod ("before sauropod") A plant-eating dinosaur that lived before the sauropods in Late Triassic and Early Jurassic times. *See* Prosauropoda in the guide.

Reconstruction ("building-up again") A model or drawing that shows what a dinosaur may have looked like.

Reptile ("crawler") A cold-blooded scaly four-legged animal that lays eggs on land. Living reptiles include snakes, turtles, and crocodiles.

Sandstone A sedimentary rock made from hardened sands deposited in an ancient river, sea, or desert.

The giant arms of *Deinocheirus* (*see page 55*). Each arm was much longer than the height of a man.

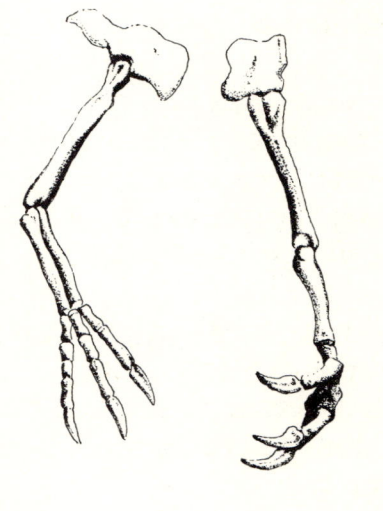

171

Saurischian ("lizard-hipped") A meat-eating or large four-legged plant-eating dinosaur. *See* Saurischia in the guide.

Sauropod ("reptile foot") A large plant-eating dinosaur with a long neck and a long tail, such as *Diplodocus* or *Apatosaurus*. Lived in the Jurassic or Cretaceous. *See* Sauropod in the guide.

Sauropodomorpha ("reptile-foot form") A long-necked, plant-eating dinosaur, either a prosauropod or a sauropod. *See* Sauropodomorpha in the guide.

Sedimentary rock A kind of rock that has formed from mud or sand, such as sandstone or limestone.

Segnosaur ("slow reptile") A strange kind of meat-eating dinosaur. *See* Segnosauria in the guide.

Skeleton The bony framework that holds your body up (and which held up the bodies of the dinosaurs).

Skull The bones of the head which support the face and protect the brain, eyes, nose, ears, and mouth.

Species A group of animals which all look the same and can breed with one another.

Stegosaur ("plated reptile") An armored dinosaur with bony plates on its back such as *Stegosaurus* and *Kentrosaurus*. *See* Stegosauria in the guide.

Suborder A group of animals or plants that is smaller than an order.

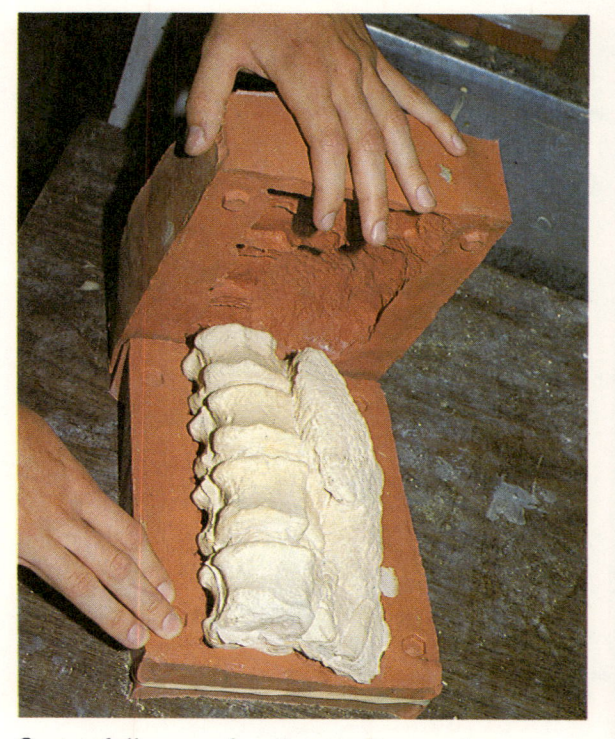

Casts of dinosaur fossils are often made so that specimens can be displayed in other museums. Here, three vertebrae, cast in hard plastic, are being taken out of a rubber mold.

Theropod ("beast foot") A meat-eating dinosaur, such as *Coelophysis*. *See* Theropoda in the guide.

Tree-fern A primitive kind of giant fern that looked like a tree.

Triassic ("three parts") The first geological period in the "age of the dinosaurs," from 245 to 208 million years ago. The name "Triassic" refers to the fact that this period is divided into three parts.

Vertebra A simple bone in the backbone. The backbone is made up of many *vertebrae*.

INDEX

Numbers in italic refer to illustrations.

A

Abelisaurus 18; skull of *18*
Acanthopholis 19, *19, 27*
Acrocanthosaurus 20
Alamosaurus 20
Albertosaurus 21, *21*
Allosaurus 22, *22, 40*
Ammosaurus 23
Anatosaurus 24, *24, 105*
Anchiceratops 25
Anchisaurus 25, *25, 121*
Ankylosauria (suborder) 26–7, *26, 27*
Ankylosaurus 27, 28, *28–9*; tail club of *28*
Antarctosaurus 29
Antrodemus (= Allosaurus) 22
Apatosaurus 30, *30, 128*
Archaeopteryx 156
Avaceratops 31, *31*
Avimimus 32

B

Bagaceratops 32
Barapasaurus 32
Barosaurus 33, *33*
Baryonyx 34, *34*
birds, origin of 156
Bonaparte, Dr. Jose 113
"bone wars:" Cope V. Marsh 14
bones, protection of *171*
Brachiosaurus 35, *128, 162, 167*; skull of *35*
Brachyceratops 36
Brachylophosaurus 36, *36*
Brontosaurus (= Apatosaurus) 30, *30*
Brown, Barnum 13, 77
Buckland, Professor William, earliest
    discoveries described by 15

C

Camarasaurus 37, *37, 128*
Camptosaurus 38, *38*
Carcharodontosaurus 39; teeth from *39*
Carnegie, Andrew 12, 60
Carnosauria (infraorder) *40, 41, 41*
Cenozoic era 10, *11*
Ceratopsia (infraorder) 42, *42, 43*
Ceratosaurus 40, 44, *44*
Cetiosaurus 45, *45, 128*

Chasmosaurus 46; skull of *46*
Claosaurus 46
classification of dinosaurs 8, *9*
Coelophysis 47, *47, 49*
Coelurosauria (infraorder) 48, *48, 49*
Coelurus 50; skull of *50*
collectors 6, 7, 12–13, *14*
color codes for suborders 16
Compsognathus 49, 51, *51*
continents, drift of 10, *10*
Cope, Edward *14*, 46, 63, 92, 159
Corythosaurus 52, *52–3*

D

Dacentrurus 53, *145*; hip girdle of *53*
Daspletosaurus 54, *54*
Datousaurus 55
Deinocheirus 55, 100
Deinonychosauria (infraorder) 56–57, *56, 57*
Deinonychus 57, 58, *58*
Dicraeosaurus 59
Dilophosaurus 59
Dinosaur, origin of name 15
Diplodocus 13, 60, *60, 128*
Douglass, Earl 13
Dravidosaurus 61
Dromaeosaurus 61; skull of *61*
Dryosaurus 62, *62, 105*
Dryptosaurus 63
Dyoplosaurus 63

E

Earth, history of the 10, *11*; era of Dinosaurs
    16, *17*
Edmontosaurus 64, *64*
Elaphrosaurus 65, *65, 101*
Erlikosaurus (= Segnosaurus?) 137
Euhelopus 66
Euoplocephalus (= Dyoplosaurus?) 63
Euskelosaurus 66
evolution, stages of 10, *11*

F

Fabrosaurus 67, *67*
family (classification of dinosaurs) 8, *9*
fossil hunters 6, 7, 12–13, *14*
fossils, formation of 7, *7*
Fox, Rev. William 75

G
Gallimimus 68, *68*, *101*
genus names, use of 8, *9*
Geranosaurus 69
glossary 169–72
Gorgosaurus (= albertosaurus) 21
Goyocephale 69

H
Hadrosaurus 70, *70*
Halticosaurus 71; skull of *71*
Hayden, Ferdinand 92
Heterodontosaurus 72, *105*
hip bone arrangement, division into orders by 8, *8*
Homalocephale 72
Hortalotarsus (= Anchisaurus) 25
Hulsanpes 56
Huxley, Professor T. H. 75
Hylaeosaurus 27, 73, *73*
Hypacrosaurus 74; skull of *74*
Hypselosaurus 74
Hypsilophodon 75, *75*, *105*

I
Iguanodon 76, *76*; origin of name 15
Indosuchus 77; skull of *77*
infraorders 8, *9*
Ischisaurus 78
Itemirus 78

J
Janensch, Werner 13
Jensen, Jim 151

K
Kentrosaurus 79, *79*, 145

L
Laelaps (= Dryptosaurus) 63
Lambeosaurus 80, *80*; skull of *80*
Leidy, Joseph 53, 70
Leptoceratops 81; skull of *81*
Lesothosaurus (= Fabrosaurus?) 67
Lexovisaurus 82, *82*
Lufengosaurus 83, *83*, *121*
Lull, R. S. 98
Lycorhinus 84

M
Maiasaura 84–5, 85; nest and eggs of *85*
Majungatholus 86
Mamenchisaurus 86–7, *87*
Mantell, Dr. Gideon *14*, 15, 73, 114
Mantell, Mrs. Mary *14*, 15
map, world, of finds *12–13*
Marsh, Othniel *14*, 30, 46, 50, 98, 103, 159
Massospondylus 88, 88
Matley, Dr. Charles 77
Megalosaurus 40, 89, *89*; origin of name 15
Melanorosaurus 90, *90–1*, *121*
Mesozoic era 10, *11*
Minmi 91; backbone of *91*
Monoclonius 92, *92*
museums, directory of 166–8
Mussaurus 93, 93
Muttaburrasaurus 93

N
Nemegtosaurus 94, *94–5*
Noasaurus 95; slashing claw of *95*
Nodosaurus 27, 96, *96*

O
Omeisaurus (= Euhelopus?) 66
Omosaurus armatus (= Dacentrurus) 53
Opisthocoelicaudia 97, *97*
orders, division into 8, *9*
Ornithischia (order) 98
Ornitholestes 49, 99, *99*
Ornithomimosauria (infraorder) 100, *100*, *101*
Ornithomimus 101, *102*, 103
Ornithopoda (suborder) 98, *103*, 104, *104*, *105*
Ouranosaurus 106, *106*
Oviraptor 107, *107*
Owen, Sir Richard *14*, 53, 88

P
Pachycephalosauria (suborder) 108, *108*, *109*
Pachycephalosaurus 109, 110, *110*
Pachyrhinosaurus 111
Paleozoic era 10, *11*
Panoplosaurus 111
Parasaurolophus 105, 112, *112*
Parksosaurus 113
Patagosaurus 113

Pectinodon 131
Pelorosaurus 114; tooth of *114*
Pentaceratops 43, 115, *115*
Phanerozoic period of evolution 10
Piatnitzkysaurus 116, *116*
Pinacosaurus 117; skull of *117*
Plateosaurus 118, *118*, *121*
Plot, Dr. Robert *14*
Polacanthus 19, 73
Precambrian era 10, *11*
Procompsognathus 49, 119, *119*
Prosaurolophus 119; skull of *119*
Prosauropoda (infraorder) 120, *120*, *121*
Protiguanodon (= *Psittacosaurus*) 123
Protoceratops 43, 122, *122*
Psittacosaurus 43, 123, *123*

R
Rhoetosaurus 124

S
Saltasaurus 124
Saltopus 125, *125*
Saurischia (order) 126, *126*
Saurolophus 127, *127*
Saurophagus (= *Acrocanthosaurus?*) 20
Sauropoda (infraorder) *128*, 129, *129*
Sauropodomorpha (suborder) 130, *130*
Saurornithoides 131; skull of *131*
Scelidosaurus 132, *132*, 145
scientific names 8, *9*
Scutellosaurus 133, *133*
Secernosaurus 134; hip bone of *134*
Segisaurus 135, *135*
Segnosauria (infraorder) 136–7, *136*
Segnosaurus 137, 138; hip bone of *138*
Shantungosaurus 139, *139*, 168
Shunosaurus 140, *140*
Silvisaurus 27, 141, *141*
species, names of, use of 8, *9*
Spinosaurus 40, 142, *142*
Staurikosaurus 143, *143*
Stegoceras 143
Stegosauria (suborder) 144, *144*, *145*
Stegosaurus *145*, 146, *146*
Stenonychosaurus 57, 147, *147*
Sternberg, Charles 13, 113
Struthiomimus 148, *148*

Struthiosaurus *101*, 149; armor plates of *149*;
    bony spine of *149*
Styracosaurus 43, 150, *150* suborders 8, *9*;
    color codes 16; division into 16, *17*
"*Supersaurus*" 151, *162*; shoulder blade of
    151
Syntarsus 49, 152, *152*

T
tallest dinosaurs compared *162*
Tarbosaurus 153; skull of *153*
Thecodontosaurus 154, *154*
Therizinosaurus 155; arm and claw of *155*
Theropoda (suborder) 156, *156*
time chart of Earth's history *11*
Titanosaurus 157; arm bone of *157*; shoulder
    girdle of *157*
Torosaurus 158; skull of *158*
Triceratops 43, 159, *159*
Troodon 160
Tsintaosaurus 160
Tyrannosaurus 40, 161, *161*; hip bones of 6, 7
Tyrannosaurus rex: as example of
    classification method 8–9, *9*

U
"*Ultrasaurus*" 162, *162*

V
Velociraptor 57, 163, *163*
Vulcanodon 164, *164*

X
Xiaosaurus 165
Xuanhanosaurus 165

Z
Zephyrosaurus 165

This short index lists all the entries by **continent**.

Africa
    Triassic 66, 88, 90, 152
    Jurassic 35, 45, 59, 67, 69, 72, 79, 84
    Cretaceous 39, 65, 86, 106, 142.

America, North
    Triassic 25, 47, 99
    Jurassic 22–3, 30, 33, 35, 37, 44, 50, 59,
        60, 133, 146, 151, 162
    Cretaceous 20–1, 24–5, 28, 31, 36, 38, 46,
        52, 54, 58, 61–4, 70, 74, 85, 92,
        96, 102–3, 110–12, 115, 119,
        127, 135, 141, 147, 148, 150,
        158–61

America, South
    Triassic 25, 78, 93, 143

Jurassic 72, 113, 116
Cretaceous 18, 29, 124, 134, 157, 164

Asia
    Triassic 83
    Jurassic 32, 55, 61, 72, 87, 140, 165
    Cretaceous 32, 55, 61, 68, 69, 72, 77, 78,
        94, 97, 107, 117, 121, 122, 127,
        138, 139, 143, 153, 155, 157,
        160, 163

Australasia
    Jurassic 124
    Cretaceous 91, 93

Europe
    Triassic 51, 71, 118, 119, 125, 132
    Jurassic 45, 53, 82, 89, 114, 154
    Cretaceous 34, 38, 73, 74, 75, 76, 116, 149,
    157

ACKNOWLEDGMENTS

The publishers wish to thank the following for kindly supplying photographs for this book:

Page 6 Michael Benton; 13 Imitor; 14 (all) Imitor; 15 Mary Evans Picture Library; 167 Pat Morris; 168 Xinhua News Agency; 172 Michael Benton.